**THINK
thin**®

THINK
thin ®

BY MURRAY J. SIEGEL &
DOLORES VAN KEUREN

PAUL S. ERIKSSON
Middlebury, Vermont

First Printing - November, 1971
Second Printing - September, 1972
Third Printing - October, 1973
Fourth Printing - June, 1974
Fifth Printing - June, 1975
Sixth Printing - August, 1976
Seventh Printing - July, 1977
Eighth Printing - December, 1978
Ninth Printing - October, 1979
Tenth Printing - February, 1981 (First Paperback)
Eleventh Printing - April, 1982 (Paper)
Twelfth Printing - April, 1984 (Paper)
Thirteenth Printing - April, 1986 (Paper)
Fourteenth Printing - April, 1988 (Paper)
Fifteenth Printing - March, 1990 (Paper)
Sixteenth Printing - October, 1996 (Paper)

TO ALL WHO ARE FAT AND FAILURE-
ORIENTED *unnecessarily*

TABLE OF CONTENTS

Think Thin®Menus

Think Thin®Recipes

FOREWORD

This guidebook to permanent slimness may be the most important book you have ever picked up in your life, because your appearance, your happiness, your health, and even your very life are involved.

Its approach is not the usual "diet" to lose weight. You have probably tried all of those—and look where *that* got you. This book is a unique and, we think, wonderful explanation of facts, simply presented and not in any way tricky or deceptive. If you will follow its signposts, you will become slimmer, healthier, happier. What more can you want?

There is a right way and a wrong way to think about food and eating, and there is a wrong way and a right way to eat. The right way is a technique that can easily be learned. If you really want to be permanently slim, you can use your intellect to learn how to eat and enjoy fresh, wholesome, colorful meals. Diets are dull. Bland. Boring. Gray. "Think Thin" eating is attractive, super-enticing, and stimulating to the palate. The recipes and menus that make up the second half of this guidebook are truly gourmet.

This may sound the same as all that other confusing and conflicting information you've acquired over the years. *It isn't!* Thinking Thin doesn't mean eating *less*. It means eating *differently*. You can acquire a permanent lifetime habit of proper thinking and eating that will enhance your life. The fun of enjoying your meals will still be there. In fact, it will probably be increased, and added to it will be all the wonderful benefits of slimness and good health.

You can re-evaluate, re-educate, and recondition your thinking. Changing your thinking will lead to changing your eating, and that in turn will change the way you look and feel. If you're overweight, you can travel with us to slim, healthy happiness. And if you're slim, and don't ever want to get fat, join us!

Murray J. Siegel
Dolores van Keuren

Freeport, N.Y.
May, 1971

INTRODUCTION

Murray Siegel was a fat baby, a fat child, a fat teenager, and a fat adult. By the time he was forty years of age, he habitually over-indulged himself with foods proper and improper and had gluttonously gorged himself up to a horrifying weight of three hundred and seventy-nine pounds. People made constant fun of him, and his own family was ashamed of his appearance. He huffed and puffed his way through life, really only half alive. He describes his existence then as a "chamber of horrors," yet despite the discomforts, the insults, and the indignities, he seemed powerless to help himself. Every Monday morning for years he started a diet to lose weight, but he was never able to stick to it past noon of the same day.

Failure-oriented, confused, and defeated, as almost all overweight people are, he made the rounds of the doctors' offices, the health cults, the exercise classes, and the diet clubs. You name it, he tried it. Occasionally, he lost some weight, but he inevitably gained it back with a bonus. At last he became sick and tired and fed up with the rigors he was continually putting himself through, and he gave up. He was also sick and tired and fed up with being grossly obese, but he was convinced he was doomed. He was fat. He had always been fat. He would always be fat. Period.

But his subconscious had not really thrown in the

sponge, because he grew curious about the terrible disease from which he suffered. He read every book on obesity that the library contained. He waded through magazines, periodicals, pamphlets, and newspapers, seeking information about overweight. He talked to fat people, to thin people, to doctors, to psychologists. In this way, he became aware of the awful confusion that surrounds the subject of overweight. Every authority had a different and conflicting idea of how to handle a weight problem. Sifting through everything to find the facts, he casually began to apply to himself some of the concepts that seemed to him to make sense. He found city, state, and federal government publications excellent sources of nutritional information. He took some of this, a little of that, and a lot of the other, until he had devised a pattern of sensible and different thinking and eating for himself. In effect, he educated himself out of his terrible obesity. In a little less than eight months, Murray J. Siegel shed not quite two hundred pounds. That was some years ago, and he is today a slim, dynamic, and energetic individual.

He became convinced that it is totally unnecessary for anyone to be fat. Dedicated to the idea of helping other poor sick overweight people, he gave up a lucrative business and founded an organization to help the overweight. This organization, known as THINK THIN, INCORPORATED, today has numerous branches to which people come from far and wide.

Thinking Thin is, in truth, a kind of philosophy, and persons attending Think Thin classes learn how to handle their own individual problems, how to be selective, how to put their eating back into proper perspective, and mainly, how to think *first*. The authorities can and do differ in their various approaches to the overweight problem, but all sources emphatically agree about one thing: the *only* way to a permanent weight loss is to re-educate and/or rehabilitate one's attitude about eating, just as Murray J. Siegel did.

Dolores van Keuren was brought up in a family whose eating habits were basically excellent. The family members were fond of vegetables, fruits, and salads. Rich desserts and fattening snacks rarely appeared on the table. Combined with these inherited good eating habits were an active metabolism and a good deal of nervous energy. Consequently, she maintained a slim, normal weight for many years without even thinking about it. However, at age thirty-five, a combination of factors caused her to begin to gain weight. Having suffered a minor accident which forced her to spend an entire summer sitting or lying around, she was denied her normal activity pattern, and, bored, began subtly to alter her eating habits. Confined, she welcomed visitors bearing cake boxes and ice cream cartons. Her good eating habits gradually became submerged in this new liking for junk foods. Soon she was faced with almost thirty extra pounds, and she discovered to her horror that they seemed almost impossible to lose. At thirty-five, her metabolism and activity patterns were no longer quite what they had been.

Discouraged, she took diet pills and did lose some weight which she quickly regained as soon as she stopped the pills, which were making her nervous and irritable. Then fate stepped in, in the form of Murray Siegel. He was the talk of the town with his astounding loss of nearly two hundred pounds. He had also worked successfully with a young boy who had shed seventy-five pounds, helped by Murray Siegel's guidance and personal example. Much impressed with these achievements, Dolores van Keuren became the third "Think Thinner," so to speak. By following Murray Siegel's advice and suggestions, she was able to lose twenty-eight pounds in exactly six weeks. She has maintained this loss ever since and enthusiastically endorses the Think Thin concept.

This book, and one preceding it, *How To Be Suddenly Slim,* came into being because of this association of the authors. It is their conviction that *permanent* weight loss *can* be achieved by anyone who is fed up enough with the indignities and the discomforts of being overweight.

Each time Murray Siegel began another unsuccessful dieting attempt, the diet itself always seemed restrictive, bland, and dull. To him, diet began to signify deprivation and cottage cheese; rigidity and self-denial. This attitude inevitably led to rapid failure because it provided him with yet another fat excuse: "This diet is *so boring!* That must be why I can't stick to it!"

He kept this in mind during his wonderful transformation from miserable fat man to happy slim man and began to develop a whole different concept of diet and cooking. This new approach made the whole thing more comfortable and more effective for him. Here were viable solutions to the eating problems that had been plaguing him for years! He discovered that a sensible, varied, and interesting method of eating to lose weight did not have to be boring at all. On the contrary, he found it could be challenging and exciting, as well as being a terrific assist to his "think" procedure.

Dolores van Keuren learned that these Think Thin

methods of food preparation and cooking enabled her to maintain her slimness with no difficulty whatever. At THINK THIN, INC., new recipes, new hints, and new suggestions are constantly forthcoming from interested class members, and that is how part of this book was compiled. We congratulate and thank every one of these contributors.

The Authors

THINK thin®

THINK
thin®
MANUAL

1. IT'S NEVER TOO LATE

Are you fed up enough with being overweight? Are you sick and tired of wearing size fifty-four trousers or a size twenty-four-and-a-half dress? Are you afraid to go to the beach? Does your doctor insist that your poor health is due to your overweight? Do you flinch when friends or relatives make sly comments about your size? Do you hate yourself and despise the way you look and the way you feel? If you are disgusted *enough* with all of these things, then you are really ready to do something constructive about your weight problem. You are sufficiently motivated, and that is the necessary prime requisite. You can stop crying on the inside while you're laughing on the outside and start being proud of yourself! You can learn to make a permanent change in your thinking, your eating, and your appearance. Let's begin!

In a broad and general sense, overweight people all fit into one of three basic categories. In the first group are those who swear they must have been born fat. For as long as they can remember, they have struggled unsuccessfully with weight problems. They have visited all the doctors, swallowed all the pills, tried all the nutty fad diets that came along, and they are still fat. They have exhausted themselves on exercise machines, jogged for miles, joined gyms and health clubs, and they are *still* fat. Most of them have just about given up and have more or less resigned themselves to being fat forever.

In the second category are the people who throughout childhood and early adulthood were lucky members of the slim society. Unaccountably, at least to themselves, they have gradually developed some kind of weight problem. Their life styles may have changed in some way. The college athlete, for example, becomes a deskbound office worker. The children grow up, and the young, active mother becomes a woman of leisure with plenty of time to sit at the bridge table. Then too, as happens with everyone, they have become a little older, a little slower. The body chemistry slows down, and those paltry five extra pounds are soon ten extra pounds. Fat piles on fat, and there they are. Some frightening simple arithmetic will demonstrate that if one manages to keep weight gains down to only five pounds a year, at the end of ten years, fifty pounds will have been gained!

In the third category are those overweight persons who actually do suffer from a glandular deficiency or a glandular imbalance of some kind. Most overweight people would like to believe that they belong to this group, but the sad truth is that they do not. According to the latest statistics, fewer than two overweight persons out of a hundred have glandular difficulties, and they might be considered the lucky ones, because modern medicine can solve their problems in short order. Their numbers grow smaller each year as endocrinological knowledge and techniques improve. Persons in this category do not concern us here. This book has been written for the other two groups—those who are fat mainly because they are consuming more than their bodies can burn up. They do not necessarily need to eat less, but they do need to learn to eat differently.

The very first step of all for would-be reducers should be a thorough physical examination by a qualified physician. Most doctors are delighted to learn that their patients intend to try to shed excess poundage! Then, before embarking on an individual eating project and before making use of the menus, recipes, and suggestions in this book, the overweight person should first begin to adjust his thinking about himself and about food and eating in general.

Unfortunately, modern life is increasingly led in a food-oriented climate. TV commercials, magazine ads, billboards, and radio announcements urge the public to eat, eat, eat! Going "out to dinner" has become a favorite American sport. Airlines scream competitively, not about their safety records, but about the delectable food the passenger can consume while flying. People seem constantly to be eating—while they bowl, while they watch a movie, while they attend a ballgame. More and more emphasis on eating and drinking attends every social function today.

Now this presents no problem to the lucky slim person who can handle all this. He's never had any difficulties and all this food just isn't particularly significant to him. But for the poor fatso, whose ideas about eating are already totally out of perspective, this incessant involvement with food makes losing weight harder and harder, if not impossible, as he bends and sways under all these social pressures.

Consequently, many fat people suffer from an erroneous subconscious equation notion:

Social life = food
Business life = food
Family life = food
Anything and everything = food

In actuality, food means none of these things. Eating is a more or less regular instinctive and enjoyable function we perform to satisfy hunger and maintain life and energy. Note the use of the word "enjoyable." Normally slim people feel legitimately hungry and legitimately enjoy satisfying that hunger. But the obese turn this quite normal enjoyment into something more. They "love" ice cream. They "adore" cake. Here again is distorted perspective. We eat to satisfy hunger and to sustain the body. Eating should ideally be no more than this. Some diet clubs call their diets a "Way of life." Wrong! Eating is a part of life, indeed, but it is not life itself. The overweight person's view of eating is often so grossly out of focus that food becomes both a reward and a penalty and thus the answer to everything. But this out-of-perspective attitude *can* be corrected by reconditioning.

Motivation is the key. If you are fed up enough with the myriad penalties of being overweight, you *can* get slim. When the desire to be slim exceeds the desire for the undisciplined consumption of enemy foods, one can eventually reverse the compulsion to eat stupidly to a compulsion to be slim.

In the opinion of the authors, there is no such thing as a mass blanket diet effective for one and all. The individual must tailormake an eating pattern for himself, based on foods (but not enemy foods) that he or she likes to eat. Learning to select and substitute proper nutritional foods for the junk food to which most fat people are addicted is part of the answer. For the convenience and assistance of readers, the eating outline followed by Murray Siegel himself is offered in the Appendix at the end of this book.

Careful reading and use of this book will be invaluable. The reader can learn how to plan sensible, satisfying menus; how to balance food intake without counting calories; how to understand and apply the importance of variation. Varying all foods is a most significant point. If lamb chops, string beans, lettuce and tomato salad, and broiled grapefruit are consumed for four nights in a row, by the fifth night the dieter will be terribly bored with this particular meal. Boredom is dangerous, because it can lead to cheating with enemy items! Even more important, we have found that if meals are repetitious, the body seems to slow down and weight is lost more slowly. The body apparently seems to burn fat more efficiently if the fuel it receives is constantly varied. Variation of foods also serves to balance and equalize the calorie level throughout each week. It insures that you get all food elements you require.

And speaking of calories, it is important to understand that while calories *do* indeed count, they cannot really be counted in a meaningful and accurate way. For example, let us assume that a single potato chip has a value of ten calories. But there are potato chips the size of a quarter, and there are potato chips as large as the diameter of a teacup. Obviously, there must then be a calorie difference, too, yet the overweight calorie counter will usually select the larger chip and convince himself that he is consuming a mere ten calories. Magnify this kind of situation throughout a day of eating, and it will be readily apparent that the

9

dieter, while believing that he has ingested perhaps
only one thousand calories, will probably have consumed much more than that.

Then, too, some calorie-counting charts are far from
dependable, as those published by varying sources often
give slightly differing values for the same foods. In
any case, even if you were a superb mathematician and
could actually obtain a completely accurate calorie count,
you would still be confronted with the greatest pitfall
of all in calorie counting. If you were trying to adhere
to a one thousand calorie a day reducing diet, it would
be quite possible to use up those thousand calories in
just two hot fudge sundaes, and that is just what many
dieters do! Weight can, of course, be lost in this way,
but it never stays off because nothing has been learned
and nothing has been changed. Rounding out your
meals with *unlimited* food items (*See* Food Categories,
Think Thin Menus section) is less demanding arith-
metically and far more efficacious in the long run than
any kind of calorie counting. *Unlimited* foods are exactly that—UNLIMITED. You can eat all you want
because these foods have little significant calorie value,
yet are loaded with nutrition. Your hunger will be
satisfied, and you'll be accomplishing something else:
you'll be turning your body chemistry on to the good
taste of these nutritious and unlimited foods while you
are losing weight. And that means a *permanent* weight
loss, since you will be changing both your thinking
and your body chemistry. You will be learning to LIKE
the foods that can keep you slim.

It is impractical to consider counting calories, or
drinking liquid diet preparations, or taking drugs for
the rest of your life. As long as you live, in order to stay

alive, you will have to eat, so the only permanent and sensible approach is to learn *how* to eat. And if you confine yourself to the proper Food Categories, the calories will count themselves! Thinking thin is a simple and effective road to permanent weight loss.

Whether you've fought a weight problem for years or have recently acquired one, it's never too late to start to do something about it. You *can* learn to make a permanent change in your thinking and eating habits. This book can point the way!

2. THE BASIC TOOLS AND HOW TO USE THEM

A person who really wants to live does not blindfold himself, put his fingers in his ears, and lie down to sleep on a railroad track. Yet in effect, this is what many confused overweight people are doing. But you must listen; you must look; you must try; you must think!

We will not rationalize or sugarcoat. We will speak the facts as we know the facts to be. It may not always be what you want to hear, but it is what you *must* hear in order to save yourself. If we sound overdogmatic at times, it is because we are trying to jolt you out of your lethargic fat rut. That rut is not only embarrassing and uncomfortable, it can literally kill you.

The first important fact is this: it is totally unnecessary to be overweight. In this chapter you will find the basic tools to help get you up off that railroad track, up out of that rut. This is a new, now approach, with logical guidelines and supplies to aid you in analyzing your present nutritional position. Let's evaluate and take stock, so that you can establish a food plan and begin to build momentum on your way to slimness.

On the pages below you will find a Check List of obvious enemy food items, with matching blank columns headed Check and Review respectively. The items on the List are, in the main, empty-caloried and low in nutritional values. They are all incorrect foods for people who wish to embark on a weight-losing project. They are also

CHECK LIST

NAME ————————————— DATE ————

Item	*Check*	*Review*
1. Ice cream	———	———
2. Cookies	———	———
3. Layer cake	———	———
4. Pie	———	———
5. Danish pastry	———	———
6. Other cakes	———	———
7. Chocolate candy	———	———
8. Other candies	———	———
9. Gravy	———	———
10. Potato chips	———	———
11. Pretzels	———	———
12. Fritos	———	———
13. Corn chips	———	———
14. Crackers	———	———
15. Mayonnaise	———	———
16. Ketchup	———	———
17. Sour cream	———	———
18. Sweet cream	———	———
19. Cold cereals	———	———
20. Hot cereals	———	———
21. Rye bread	———	———

Item	Check	Review
22. Whole wheat bread	_____	_____
23. Pumpernickel	_____	_____
24. Bagels	_____	_____
25. Rolls	_____	_____
26. Italian bread	_____	_____
27. Biscuits	_____	_____
28. Muffins	_____	_____
29. Spaghetti	_____	_____
30. Macaroni	_____	_____
31. Noodles	_____	_____
32. Rice	_____	_____
33. Corn	_____	_____
34. Baked beans	_____	_____
35. Prunes	_____	_____
36. Lima beans	_____	_____
37. Figs	_____	_____
38. Dried apricots	_____	_____
39. Raisins	_____	_____
40. Bananas	_____	_____
41. Cherries	_____	_____
42. Watermelon	_____	_____
43. Avocado	_____	_____
44. Grapes	_____	_____
45. Dates	_____	_____
46. French fries	_____	_____
47. Baked potato	_____	_____
48. Mashed potato	_____	_____
49. Honey	_____	_____
50. Maple syrup	_____	_____
51. Roast pork	_____	_____
52. Ham	_____	_____
53. Bacon	_____	_____

Item	*Check*	*Review*
54. Sausages	___	___
55. Salami	___	___
56. Pastrami	___	___
57. Corned beef	___	___
58. Bologna	___	___
59. Liverwurst	___	___
60. Nuts	___	___
61. Yogurt	___	___
62. Butter	___	___
63. Chinese food	___	___
64. Pizza	___	___
65. French dressing	___	___
66. Russian dressing	___	___
67. Roquefort dressing	___	___
68. Lox	___	___
69. Gefilte fish	___	___
70. Smoked whitefish	___	___
71. Herring	___	___
72. Sturgeon	___	___
73. Puddings	___	___
74. Peanut butter	___	___
75. Jelly or jam	___	___
76. Beer	___	___
77. Hard liquor	___	___
78. Wine	___	___
79. Cooking oils	___	___
80. ___	___	___
81. ___	___	___
82. ___	___	___
83. ___	___	___
84. ___	___	___
85. ___	___	___

THE BASIC TOOLS AND HOW TO USE THEM

universally the foods that fat people unfortunately prefer. Over-indulgence in these foods, often to the near exclusion of other, more sensible and nutritious foods, is one of the reasons that overweight people are overweight. All of the foods on the Check List are absolutely prohibited during the period of weight loss.

However, it is most important to know exactly what types of foods you are currently eating, because you cannot correct your nutritional errors unless you are thoroughly aware of what your errors are. Read the List over carefully and, in the Check column, mark those items which you like very much at present. Be sure to check all the items you currently care for, whether you actually allow yourself to eat them or not. Note the blanks at the end of the List for any items that may appeal to you but are not on the List. Be completely honest in checking your preferences.

During the course of your weight-losing project, make a periodic review of this Check List in the following manner (We suggest a review every six weeks.):

On a separate piece of paper, write down all the items you can remember checking on the date you originally filled out the Check List. Don't try to think of items you are not now allowed to eat and assume that you must have checked them, but honestly attempt to perform a memory recall. Now get out the Check List and place it next to the piece of paper. In the Review column, check all items that you have remembered and listed on the sheet of paper. As these six-weeks checks proceed, if you have abstained (that means to do *entirely* without!) from your original preferences, your list of recall should diminish. If it does not, you've been cheating! And even a tiny taste is a cheat. There are no small murders, you know. The victim is dead, whether he has been shot with a single bullet or a whole belt of machine gun ammunition! Nor can a woman be a little bit pregnant. She is, or she isn't! In the same way, there are no little cheats. If you really want to be slim, there can be no compromises. A determined attitude about this makes the whole thing easier in the long run.

This Check List forms a part of the Think Thin philosophy. We refer to it as the "Fat Recall." In the beginning, overweight people consider the enemy items on the Check List to be legitimate foods, when they are in fact really junk foods. As your recall of these items becomes less accurate, it means they are becoming less and less important to you, and this is proof that your attitude is changing. Although the items on the Check List are completely forbidden while you are engaged in losing weight, they are only temporarily forbidden. They will definitely be allowable, *if you still want them,* on your self-supervised maintenance project, in quantities that you will have learned how to handle without detriment to the maintenance of your new slimness.

In the Menus section toward the back of this book you will find how Murray J. Siegel and Dolores van Keuren followed an eating project for personal success in their weight-loss attempts. A section of "Food Categories," follows. For maximum weight loss in minimum time, these two sections are good frameworks to guide you, but as individuals differ widely, you should tailor-make an eating project to fit yourself and your own individual preferences in selecting foods.* In doing this, it is wise to enlist the aid of your physician. Government

*Note: *Foods are: Meat, poultry, fish, eggs, cheese, skim milk, bread, fruits, and vegetables.*

18

nutritional pamphlets can also be a valuable aid. These pamphlets are available in your local public library, or the Department of Health in Washington, D.C. will send them to you on request.

Perform a nutritional self-analysis as the authors did. Unfortunately, overweight people are rarely willing to take the time to do so, but their undisciplined, slipshod, hideous eating habits must be scientifically altered until they are acutely aware of the extent of their nutritional imbalance. This awareness and therefore honesty are prerequisites of becoming slim and *staying* slim. So start thinking. Work out a satisfying eating project for yourself and experience the adventure and excitement of losing weight where heretofore you knew only the confusion and mystery of your own particular overweight chamber of horrors.

It's not the question of losing weight that is important. It's *how* the weight was lost that matters. The manner in which the weight was lost influences whether or not it will be possible to maintain the loss. If weight is shed by taking diet pills, or by starving, or by drinking liquid low-calorie diet preparations only, or by subscribing to an unbalanced fad diet (of which a frightening number are printed frequently in popular magazines), almost inevitably the lost weight is soon gained back, often with a bonus. This is because diet pills, starving, and fad diets are temporary shortcut methods. You cannot continue to eat or not eat that particular way for the rest of your life. When you revert to your former eating patterns, the lost pounds begin to pile back on, because nothing has really been changed, and nothing has certainly been learned. These kinds of weight-losing methods can even be downright dangerous, since they can destroy the body chemistry with consequent negative repercussions on physical well-being and on emotional well-being. The dieter has been defeated again! This leads to the failure-oriented attitude so many overweight persons have.

But if the weight is lost through satisfying, balanced, nutritional eating and the re-education of the attitudes about decent food and proper thinking, it is a different story. The lost weight can be maintained with ease and comfort. The authors and thousands of people who have undergone the Think Thin educational process are proof of that!

At the conclusion of this chapter you will find your individual Weight Record Chart. This is referred to as a Nutritional Profile.Weight losses or gains roughly indicate your adherence or non-adherence to a correct eating project to lose weight. As you record your losses and gains, you will be able to form an over-all understanding of your burning ability. It is important to understand what is meant by "burning ability." Most people seem to undergo a metabolic cycle which is not yet fully understood. For persons pursuing a weight-losing project, there are weeks when no matter how varied and balanced the food intake, the weight loss is negligible. We call this a bad burning week. Conversely, there are other weeks when a certain amount of cheating has occurred, and yet a major loss of weight takes place. This is called a good burning week. It is thought that these good or bad burning weeks may be influenced by how much physical activity has occurred, what the variations and selections of food might have been, and what the emotional state of the individual was during the week. Bodily caloric needs vary each day. All of this is, however, only theoretical at this point. In women, the menstrual cycle may also be partially involved, but since this apparent metabolic cycle occurs with men, too, that cannot be the whole story.

No matter what the exact scientific reasons, these good and bad burning weeks *do* take place. If in a given week, you have not followed your eating project exactly as planned and have deviated grossly by indulging in several highballs, two pieces of cake, and three servings of ice cream and have still lost two pounds, this indicates that that was a good burning week in which you might have lost four or five pounds had you observed your eating project properly. Should this happen to you, make a penciled notation, "G.B.," next to your recorded weight for that week. Conversely, in a bad burning week, a sizeable gain is almost guaranteed by gross deviating, and sizeable gains can be psychologically very defeating. The following conclusion must be drawn: Good burning weeks are completely unpredictable, so it behooves the dieter to observe his eating project as correctly as possible at all times in order to take full advantage of good burning weeks whenever they may occur. And be careful not to allow bad burning weeks to become a fat copout! Your weight losses should not consistently diminish. If they do, you are either losing interest, or getting sloppy about proper variation of foods, or just plain drifting. In any event, you should never reach a "plateau." When dieters are taking drugs to lose weight, a true plateau can happen. This plateau is a point at which weight loss stubbornly refuses to take place. This happens because the body chemistry adjusts to the level of drugs being ingested, and consequently, the drugs are no longer effective. Unscrupulous "diet pill" doctors can force their dieting patients off the plateau by increasing the drug dosages, a dangerous procedure at best, as testified by the American Medical Association in their investigations into the diet-pill racket. Persons following eating projects to lose weight reach false plateaus that they themselves have precipitated by drifting too far afield from their correct eating projects. They begin to cheat so much that they are consuming exactly what their bodies can burn up, and so their weight remains static. If *you* reach a point where your weight loss is unsatisfactory, take stock of your nutritional situation. Review your Check List and study your Weight Record Chart. Take a good look at what you are really eating. Remember to be a good quarterback and mix up your nutritional signals, too, so the body chemistry doesn't become bored.

How to make use of your individual Weight Record Chart, your Nutritional Profile: Weigh yourself once a week *only*, and enter your weight and your loss or gain in the appropriate columns. Weighing conditions *must be duplicated exactly*. You should weigh on the same day each week, at the same time of day, on the same scale, wearing approximately the same clothing or no clothing at all. Yet do not over-emphasize the significance of this weekly weigh-in. Many small seemingly insignificant factors influence weight at any given time. A glass of water, for example, weighs about three quarters of a pound. A normal urination excretes about three quarters of a pound of fluid. Therefore, if you drink a glass of water just before weighing this week, but do not the next week, or you urinate prior to weighing this week but do not the next week, you can easily see the effect this might have on what the scale will read. It is that critical and therefore that unimportant. Your weekly weights are merely indications of how the re-education of your attitudes is proceeding.

Do not become a slave to the scale! Let us assume that Thursday is your usual day for the weekly weigh-in. On Tuesday, having followed your eating project faithfully since the prior Thursday, you just cannot resist sneaking on your scale to see what is happening. Hooray! You have lost three pounds already this week! But the fat subconscious being what it is, the idea may occur to you that since you will not be recording your weight until Thursday, perhaps you can coast today and cheat just a little bit and still be able to record two pounds on Thursday. And that's the road back to Fatsville! Or the reverse can happen: when you step on the scale on Tuesday you discover that you have lost no weight at all, even though you have eaten correctly! The body just works that way sometimes and patience is required. But you won't feel patient! You'll feel resentful and defeated, which may trigger you into an emotional eating binge of the wrong foods. Either way, constant weighing can be severely detrimental. The only real reason that overweight people are tempted to weigh constantly is to find out how much cheating they are getting away with! So don't become a slave to the scale. Weigh only once a week. If you should cheat, jump right back on your eating project and not on the scale! Try not to be overly curious and impatient. Patience is a very real and necessary virtue in successful and permanent weight loss. The average impatient overweight individual wants an overnight instant magic miracle. There are none. It just cannot happen that way. But it *can* happen, if you will try to develop some patience along the way. In this sense, patience *is* a magic ingredient.

Along with patience, there are two other magic ingredients for successful weight loss. One of these is courage.

So many fat people give up when the going gets a little tough or a little different. You've got plenty of courage, so apply it! Don't be a quitter. And the final, most important magic ingredient is intelligence. Overweight people may be absolutely brilliant in their work, but they are sometimes notoriously stupid about their eating. Use your intelligence to interpret correctly your Weight Record Chart and become nutritionally self-analytical. Use your intelligence to think before you eat. Use your intelligence to become a selective and independent eater. Ask yourself meaningful questions, and you will be well on your way to thinking thin.

Individual Weight Record Chart
(Nutritional Profile)

DATE	WEIGHT	LOSS	DATE	WEIGHT	LOSS
		START			

DATE	WEIGHT	LOSS	DATE	WEIGHT	LOSS

3. THE THREE-MEAL-A-DAY CONCEPT (MEAL #1)

It is almost impossible to lose weight permanently without understanding and adopting the three-meal-a-day concept. To achieve success, you must plan to consume three attractive, balanced, and varied meals each day, plus, of course, as many proper between-meal snacks as you desire. When you reach maintenance, the content of your meals can perhaps change slightly, but the three-meal-a-day concept remains of paramount importance.

Proper spacing of meals is significant, but here again it is a highly individual matter. A pat set of rules just doesn't work. Everyone need not leap out of bed at six to have breakfast at seven, luncheon at one, and dinner at six. Such a requirement would be patently ridiculous. You can get slim in your own life style and should therefore figure out a meal schedule that is comfortable and workable for you.

To help you keep in mind the absolute necessity of consuming three meals each day, we prefer to call breakfast Meal #1. It can be eaten at any time, depending on your own habits, but it *must* be eaten! (If you work at night and sleep by day, as some people do, this instruction still applies. Simply alter the timing to suit your own hours.)

Overweight persons make a gross error when they skip breakfast, or Meal #1. They rarely bother with this meal for two basic reasons. First, many unwittingly become lazy and undisciplined. They prefer lying in bed a bit longer to actually planning, preparing, and consuming a breakfast meal. There is a vicious cycle involved here. The more one lies in bed, the less energy one expends, and consequently, the less food is required to maintain weight. In simpler terms, the more you sleep, the less you should eat. Fat people are usually exhausted from carrying extra pounds around, and so they are inclined to lie down more and to sleep more than slim energetic individuals do. Naturally, as they do not decrease their food intake, they inevitably get fatter and fatter. Then exhaustion increases, mobility decreases, and even the breathing shows adverse effects. Overweight people really do huff and puff their way about.

Secondly, overweight people erroneously (and often even subconsciously) assume that by skipping Meal #1 they may perhaps have more leeway to consume enemy "goodies" at the end of the day and still lose weight. This kind of thinking is the beginning of the end.

The primary rule, then, is: Meal #1 must be consumed every day! This meal is the foundation of the day upon which the two other meals are built. Activity and productivity are significantly connected with Meal #1. Research and investigation have demonstrated that physical output and mental performance are definitely not up to par when this important meal has been missed. You must put the proper fuel into the body to start efficient physical and mental operation each day.

Meal #1 should constantly be as varied and different as you can arrange. We found this to be of signal importance in losing the greatest amount of weight in the shortest possible time. Variation accomplishes three things:

1. It keeps *you* interested.

2. It keeps your body guessing so that it burns fat faster.

3. It balances calorie intake without actually counting calories.

The American idea of breakfast is rigid and habitual. If it isn't eggs, bacon, orange juice, rolls and butter, Danish, and coffee, it isn't breakfast. This concept sometimes makes it difficult for the overweight to change their thinking enough to enable them to vary Meal #1 sufficiently. They just *won't* try something different! Laughably enough, if a friend or hostess should urge them to "Start your diet tomorrow!" or "Eat the cake today!," these same dogmatic overweight individuals can suddenly become very flexible and vacillating. It is pitifully easy to influence a fat man to indulge in cake, but it is most difficult to convince the same fat man to alter his habitual stubborn concepts of Meal #1. In many parts of the world, beefsteak is common for breakfast, or fish, or even more exotic and unusual dishes. Relax your thinking about Meal #1 and be prepared to *try* something different. Remember—in obesity there is rigidity, while in slimness there is flexibility!

To help you understand how to plan your eating and how to utilize Think Thin recipes, the section called "Think Thin Menus" contains twenty-one consecutive varied menus for Meal #1 (breakfast). Related Meal #2 (luncheon) and related Meal #3 (dinner) menus will be found directly following the Meal #1 menus. Recipes for specific starred dishes will be found in the Recipe Section.

Where possible, quantities are specified, but it is the opinion of the authors that quantities are best determined by the individual. Protein (meat, fish, poultry, eggs, cheese) is the most important food category. Protein satisfies hunger best, and so each individual should experiment to discover what amounts satisfy him longest and therefore help keep him from cheating later with "enemy" foods. Obviously, a man requires slightly larger quantities than a woman, and a laborer would need more than a sedentary office worker. Weighing foods with a tiny postal scale seems juvenile. Persons attending "diet clubs" where such weighing of foods is required have been known to weigh out their proteins meticulously and then wind up the meal with strawberry shortcake and whipped cream! Thinking thin means *thinking,* and so each person should use his intelligence to determine amounts correct and satisfying for his own particular body and activity patterns.

Finally, a hint for those who insist that they just cannot consume a meal upon arising. Don't! Have fruit (perhaps a half grapefruit or half of a canteloupe) and a cup of coffee when you first get up and then later, when you are more "in gear," have a second cup of coffee (or tea) and the proper indicated balance of Meal #1.

Your menu planning cannot be done in a hit or miss style if it is to be effective. Work out a week's menus at a time, so that you can shop accordingly. Buy a slightly larger roast or turkey, etc., than the size of your family warrants in order to provide leftovers for Meal #1 and Meal #2 on succeeding days. Fruits and vegetables should also be varied from day to day.

We suggest that eggs be used as sparingly as possible. Although it is true that the white of egg is all protein, the yolk is largely fat and cholesterol. Then, eggs, being small, are not really as satisfying as meat, fish, or poultry. Use eggs only to provide good variation in your

30

menus. Be wary of using them too frequently because they are "quick and easy."

Cheese, especially the hard cheeses like American, Swiss, Cheddar, Muenster, can be another danger item. Like eggs, cheese is "quick and easy," but we have found it to be a poor burner with a considerable fat content of its own. We suggest that these cheeses be used only as occasional menu variants rather than frequently. Cheese can set yet another trap for the unwary. Because cheese is allowed in the eating pattern, the reducer may persuade himself that snacking on extra cheese is then permissible. Not so. Extra cheese adds extra calories. Don't fool yourself. Don't let cheese become your "candy."

Remember, then, that Meal #1, breakfast, sets the foundation of your nutritional day no matter when that day begins. It fuels the body properly so that it can perform well during the first hours of the day. Even more important, this crucial meal begins to set you at a high nutritional level, which will keep you more satisfied and will help prevent undisciplined "enemy" cheating later in the day. Many dieters cheat simply because they are too hungry. Then, too, many overweight people have a tendency to bank calories in reverse. They eliminate Meal #1 and deliberately consume very little lunch, feeling that because they really haven't eaten much during the day they are certainly then *entitled* to make up for it later on with either food or "enemy" food, but then, unfortunately, they often find themselves powerless to stop. Part of your understanding of yourself is to realize that you, too, may have this common tendency and to determine that you will make Meal #1 a daily required routine. Meal #1 helps guarantee total nutritional satisfaction.

4. THINK AHEAD: MEAL #2

The very same overweight people who make a habit of skipping Meal #1 are also often prone to eliminating luncheon, too, or at least skimping on it. These are the people who say, "I eat no breakfast and not much lunch. I can't understand why I have this weight problem. Really, I eat very little when you come right down to it!" What they fail to realize is that through skipping or skimping on the first two meals of the day they do appear to eat very little, but appearances are deceiving in this case. What actually happens is that they short-change themselves nutritionally, and after four o'clock or so, their bodies urgently demand sustenance. Everyone gets hungry when the body has not been fueled— domestic animals, wild animals, fat people, and even *slim* people! And so at this point, the meal-skipper begins eating—anything and everything, usually. He answers the body's demands mainly with junk foods because he is by then so hungry that he is not able to be discriminating or selective. Anything will do, the more calorie-laden the better, since those are the types of edibles to which his fat appetite is attracted. In the final analysis, although he has skipped Meal #1 and Meal #2, he winds up the day eating as much if not more than he would have by consuming these two meals, and most of his consumption has been unwisely selected.

This is *bad habit timing*. It is one reason why fat people are so notoriously unsuccessful in most of their dieting attempts. The three-meal-a-day philosophy can help to eliminate this hideous pattern. By consuming three balanced satisfying meals each day, the overweight individual can be assisted in resisting the temptation to cheat unthinkingly and stupidly later in the day. Because this late-day compulsive eating of junk foods is also an habitual conditioned reflex with most fat people, the three-meal-a-day concept is not an instant guarantee that they will immediately correct the habit. It can, however, be much more easily handled when the day's eating has been sensible and balanced. Then the chances of excess cheating become far less.

To simplify this three-meal-a-day idea, we will refer to luncheon as Meal #2, the second step in a day of good eating to lose weight. When people are dieting, this meal often has a tendency to become bland, dull, or grabbed on the run, if it is partaken at all. It need not be. It should not be. It can be interesting, satisfying, and colorful, without investing in a great deal of time or trouble. All it takes is a little thought and some imagination.

So many fat people are not willing to put in even one minute of thought or effort on Meal #2. They claim, "I just don't have time. It's quicker and easier to grab a doughnut, or some crackers, or just to forget about the meal entirely." They blame this attitude on the frantic pace of modern life, instead of on their own fat thinking, which is the real culprit. They "just don't have time!" Oddly enough, they find time to eat junk later on. "It's easier to grab a doughnut . . ." Deep inside, they know it isn't easy to be fat. Overweight people should recognize this attitude for the fat copout that it is. If you really want to be slim permanently, we maintain that you must have the time to think first and then to eat wisely.

While we certainly do not advocate major projects in the kitchen at Meal #2 time, we feel that some kind of thoughtful preparation should take place. Remember, it takes more time and effort to be fat in the long run! The easy, attractive Think Thin recipes in the Recipe Section can help you keep Meal #2 satisfying and interesting.

Meal #1 is fuel for the morning hours, and Meal #2 is fuel for the afternoon. Meal #2 is a larger meal because it must sustain you through a greater time span to Meal #3, dinner, the food pinnacle of the day. Meal #2 should be thoughtfully spaced at an interval from Meal #1 that is comfortable for you. This will naturally involve a different number of hours for different individuals.

Meal #2 should be varied from day to day and also should be varied from Meal #1 each day. This important principle of variation is well illustrated in the twenty-one consecutive days of Meal #2 menus which you will find immediately following the Meal #1 menus toward the back of this book. Complete variation in the three daily meals for twenty-one days can be easily achieved by observing the twenty-one day menus to the fullest extent. We suggest you start out by following these menus. If any of the suggestions involve foods you heartily dislike, substitute foods you do like after studying the section on Food Categories. After the twenty-one days, use your intelligence and your imagination to plan your own varied and colorful menus. Enlist the aid of the Recipe Section in doing this.

The Meal #2 menus, in the back, are directed mainly

to those who are at home each day or who can return home for this middle meal. In Chapter V, students, plant workers, and business people can find helpful suggestions to fit their own particular problems with Meal #2.

Make a proper and varied Meal #2 another habitual part of your daily routine. Don't get the false idea that if you skimp on lunch, you might lose weight faster. This is entirely erroneous! A good slogan to keep in mind is: "The less you eat (of good foods), the sooner you'll cheat (with enemy foods)." Think of your body as analogous to an automobile. If you need to travel one hundred miles, you certainly wouldn't fuel your car with only one gallon of gasoline, because then it simply would not be able to travel the full distance. Neither will your body! Keep your nutritional level high with a good middle meal, and you'll be a lot less likely to succumb to thoughtless cheating later in the afternoon.

5. LUNCH AWAY FROM HOME: MEAL #2, *continued*

Dietitians notwithstanding, school, college, hospital, industrial plant, and almost any institutional cafeterias often seem to have little or no concept of a proper, balanced luncheon menu, especially for people who are trying to lose weight and correct poor eating habits. The captive diners in these cafeterias are victims of real menu atrocities. The meats are "stretched" with bread and cereal fillers and usually are drowned in gravy; potatoes, macaronis, rice, and noodle dishes are favorite items that appear constantly; salads are skimpy, wilted, piled with gooey dressings, or non-existent; the few vegetables are creamed or drip with butter or margarine; the desserts are really calorie-freighted.

Students who must spend their lunch periods at school and employees of industrial plants who eat in company cafeterias often complain that Meal #2 presents a problem. Actually, this is often a fat copout. With a little thinking, a little intelligent planning, this meal need present no difficulty whatever. People in these situations seriously interested in permanent weight loss can manage the middle meal nicely. A difference in attitude may be required, but different doesn't necessarily mean difficult. The student, for instance, may have to get up a few minutes earlier in the morning in order to prepare the proper lunch for himself. The industrial employee may have to use his intelligence to shop wisely and to spend a short time the evening before in packing the correct lunch. We definitely believe in carrying your lunch with you if you really wish to eat properly to lose weight.

Depend on yourself. You can do it! Temporarily, until you reach the weight goal you have set yourself, determine to arise a few minutes earlier in the morning to prepare a proper lunch for yourself. Even better, plan and make the lunch the evening before. Keep it refrigerated all night and take it out to carry with you the very last thing before leaving home. This way it will be fresh when lunchtime comes around. This way you will know that you have no chance of bungling Meal #2.

Many foods are sold in supermarkets packaged in small plastic containers. We suggest keeping a stock of these plastic containers on hand in various sizes. They can be a great convenience in packing a Think Thin lunch. Rolls of tear-off plastic "baggies" are another invaluable aid, and a one-pint thermos is a good investment.

Sandwiches are no problem for men, who are allowed two slices of white bread at Meal #2. Women are allowed only one slice, but this single slice can be made into two for sandwich purposes. Toast the bread lightly and slice through with a very sharp, long-bladed knife. An instrument is now available which performs this function. Called "Serv-A-Slice," it can be purchased at department and specialty stores.

Seven sample "Take with you" lunches for students and workers are listed below in the following section. With these samples as a guide, plus a little ingenuity and the help of the Recipe Section at the back, you can plan your own lunchbox menus. The main thing is to pack a satisfying and correct meal that will carry you through comfortably until you are back at home for dinner, or Meal #3. Note the complete variation in the sample lunches. Each differs from the one before it. When planning your own, be sure that Meal #2 also varies from Meal #1 of that day as well.

Exciting Suggestions for Happy Lunch Boxes

(Asterisks refer to recipes detailed in Recipe Section. See Index for page numbers.)

Day number 1:

Medium-sized cold broiled chicken breast (prepared
    night before)
White bread (1 slice for woman, 2 for man)
Radishes
Celery sticks
Green pepper slices
Large fresh pear
Low-calorie soda
(Pack raw vegetables in plastic baggies)

Day number 2:

Thermos of hot Mushroom Soup*
Meat Loaf* sandwich
Cucumber salad in plastic container
Pineapple Ambrosia* in plastic container

Day number 3:

Tuna salad* in plastic container
White bread (1 slice for woman, 2 for man)
Thermos hot chicken bouillon

39

Carrot sticks in plastic baggie
Temple orange

Day number 4:
Thick roast beef sandwich with lettuce and mustard
Large dill pickle
Large fresh apple
Low-calorie soda

Day number 5:
Turkey sandwich with lettuce and mustard
Salad Delight* in plastic container
Fruit Compote* in plastic container
Coffee with skim milk

Day number 6:
Chopped Chicken Liver* in plastic container
White bread (1 slice for woman, 2 for man)
Small whole tomato
A few scallions in plastic baggie
Large dill pickle
Low-calorie soda

Day number 7:
Shrimp Salad* in plastic container
White bread (1 slice for woman, 2 for man)
Green pepper rings in plastic baggie
Thermos hot vegetable bouillon
Navel orange
Tea with lemon

* * *

Each of the foregoing Lunch Box Menus takes only a
few minutes to prepare. Overweight people *can* lose
weight by taking diet pills, starving, drinking liquid
diets, and so on, but their weight losses are always

temporary because they haven't changed anything, they haven't learned anything, they really haven't put forth any effort. Weight loss *will be permanent* if you can re-educate your eating habits and your attitude about eating. This whole plan must be worked at. Take the small amount of time necessary to think first and prepare yourself a proper lunchbox. Don't forget a small plastic fork and spoon and a fancy paper napkin. Then enjoy your middle meal, knowing that at the same time you are eating correctly to burn fat from your body and yet satisfy your hunger.

Businessmen and businesswomen who work in offices are sometimes subjected to special problems with the middle meal. Some overweight business people can be rather obtuse about their eating, but if they can apply a little thought to their eating difficulties, they take a major step toward slimness. All they need do is apply to their eating projects the same intelligence they use so well in other areas of their lives, especially their business lives. In competitive modern America, unintelligent people are not able to stay in business for very long. It therefore follows that business people are more than adequately equipped to handle their eating problems. How sad it is to see an otherwise smart businessman risking his health, his life, and perhaps even his business by being overweight. A good business brain is not automatic protection from misdirected thinking in the area of food and eating. If you go to business, don't let it become a fat excuse for all your eating indiscretions!

Some business people will find themselves in a position where it is perfectly possible to carry Meal #2 with them each day, as do students and plant workers. They might not be happy to hear this, but if it's all right to carry all those exhausting extra pounds around, what effort is it to carry lunch in an attaché case or purse? This would be only a temporary measure, after all, until the weight-loss goal is reached. If this is your situation, be guided by our Exciting Suggestions For Happy Lunch Boxes.

A few offices have small refrigerators and/or hot plates, which personnel are allowed to use. If so, coffee, tea, and bouillon can be prepared, and soups can be heated. This can be a helpful adjunct to Meal #2. See that you keep appropriate items in your desk drawer for use at lunch time, such as tea bags, instant coffee, bouillon cubes or powders, artificial sweetener, powdered skim milk, fresh fruits, and so on. Always be prepared. There are even offices, especially in larger companies, which boast small, but completely equipped kitchens on the business premises. If you are employed by such a firm, and you are trying to lose weight, you simply have no fat copout at all, except sheer laziness and stupidity!

The major common difficulty for business people, however, is the prevalent custom of "going out for lunch." Yet it really need not be an impassable stumbling block. Some would-be weight losers go completely to pieces when in a restaurant with clients or co-workers. Intelligence flies out the window, and they'll eat and drink almost anything. Their excuse:

"Well, it's so embarrassing to be on a diet. I look terribly peculiar not drinking or eating what everyone else is having!"

The excuse-makers should remember that it looks much more *peculiar* to be obese; it is much more *embarrassing* to bulge over your belt; it is downright *degrading* when you can't even fit into the booth at the diner! In truth, no one really cares *what* anyone else eats or drinks.

People who want to lose weight and re-educate their attitudes should strive to become independent thinkers and independent eaters. The fat person wails: "At lunch, the boss absolutely *insisted* I have the Baked Alaska!"

The motivated reducer, learning to become independent, says politely but firmly: "No, thanks. I prefer a half grapefruit."

In almost any kind of restaurant, it is possible to eat a correct and satisfying Meal #2 and lose weight at the same time. It is more than possible. It can be easy. The trick is to be selective. Go right ahead "out to lunch" with your co-workers, your boss, or your partner. Read the menu with care and SELECT a balanced and enjoyable Meal #2 that fits your individual eating project which you have worked out according to the Suggested Meal #2 Eating Pattern. Use your intelligence and your imagination.

So long as you are paying to have this meal served to you, you are certainly entitled to have it served the way you request. Most waiters and waitresses will be quite cooperative about this. Do you wish your fish broiled without butter? Then say so. Order your salad without dressing and request plain vinegar and lemon wedges served with it. Skip the potatoes and order two vegetables instead. Ignore the dessert menu and ask if fresh fruit of any kind is available. If it isn't, have an extra cup of tea or coffee while your companions have dessert. If you are a wise weight loser, you'll have an extra piece of fruit in your desk to snack on later, anyhow.

And the most important thing is—don't endlessly discuss your "diet" with co-workers or associates. They, like your family, are no doubt thoroughly bored with hearing about your weight problems. Fat people have the tendency to talk about their "diets" ad infinitum while they

43

are progressing well and losing some weight, but when they reach a stalemate, they avoid the subject, which is the signal to family and friends that they have failed again. Don't make an issue out of your eating or your eating problems. Be discreet. In the long run, your new slim figure will speak for itself!

There's another danger. Human nature being what it is, if your companions learn you have embarked on a diet, they are apt to spend the entire lunch hour trying to convince you to order foolishly and "start your diet tomorrow!" So the less said, the better. If your co-workers are slim, they just won't understand your problem, never having coped with it. If they are fat, they hate to see anyone else successfully handle a situation they themselves have failed at, and so the urging to "start tomorrow." Either that, or they will question you thoroughly, trying to find out any instant "magic" aspects that they might be able to apply to themselves.

Now, what about those "martini" lunches? That's a tough one, but it is not insoluble. Liquid business lunches are partly, of course, habit, and partly just going along with the others. If you really want to be slim, you must face the fact that, temporarily, alcoholic beverages of any kind are not for you.

If you frequently entertain clients or associates at lunch, and they are accustomed to martinis or whatever, order these drinks for them and order club soda with a twist of lemon for yourself. If your companions comment about this, don't act embarrassed. Keep in mind how much more embarrassing it is to be fat. Besides, the comments will probably be brief. People, especially business people, have more important things to think about at length than your drinking habits! But if you feel it's necessary, you can make a remark like:

"I really don't feel like having a drink today," or something to that effect, but don't harp on your diet or proclaim loudly that you are "on the wagon." This only makes a big thing out of it.

If you are paying the check, order exactly what you want. The fact that you're paying certainly gives you that prerogative! If you are being entertained at lunch and your host or hosts *insist* that they order a drink for you—let them do it! Club soda with a shot glass of gin or vodka on the side is a perfect choice. Sip the soda. Later, pour in the shot glass of gin or vodka. While you are all talking, let the drink sit there until the ice melts.

These are all merely suggestions, and perhaps you can think up maneuvers of your own. In the final analysis, you ought to remember that you really are a grownup now, and that if you want results, it's up to you.

Usually, no one really makes much comment or actually *cares* what you're drinking, so long as you hold a glass in your hand or have one in front of you. Most fat people would like to think otherwise, but that is really just another fat copout. Drinking at lunch is a habit you have cultivated over a period of time. It can be difficult to develop a new and better habit of not drinking, but it is far from impossible. If you succumb to "martini" lunches, it is because you just don't care enough about being slim. Conversely, if you really care about reaching the weight goal you have set for yourself, you can easily get around the necessity for drinking.

In other words, no one can force you to do anything you don't really want to do. Naturally your business associates are prone to urging food and drink on you. They wish to please you. And what makes an overweight person happiest? Roses? Of course not—it's food and drink. Besides, they are accustomed to seeing you gorge yourself with drinks and rich desserts. Put being slim ahead of being a pushover for your associates and friends. *Become an independent thinker and an independent eater.* This is a prerequisite for slimness.

One further thing must be discussed in conjunction with working people and their working day, and that is the famous "coffee break." This has become an American institution. It started out as a ten-minute rest period. Then it branched out into having coffee during the rest period. Then it became "coffee *and* . . ."

Coffee and coffee cake

Coffee and Danish

Coffee and doughnut

Coffee and corn muffin

Coffee and English muffin

And so on . . .

Most of the "ands" are empty-caloried items. What are empty-caloried foods? They are foods containing very little nutrition, but lots and lots of calories. People wanting to lose weight and become permanently slim should think of these kinds of foods as "enemy foods." That is exactly what they are—enemies in the battle for slimness.

Inevitably, to fat people, the "and" soon became much more important than either the coffee or the break. Think! Change a poor habit into a good habit. What's wrong with a delicious piece of crisp fresh fruit with your coffee? It's different, and it is easy to do if you bring a piece each day and keep it in your locker or desk drawer for coffee break time. There's nothing wrong with just plain coffee, either! A break from the working routine should really not signify food, anyway. The break should relax you and refresh you from business tensions. Overindulgence in enemy foods at coffee break time can contribute to a feeling of sluggishness.

6. THE NUTRITIONAL PINNACLE: MEAL #3

It is dinner time. The table is set and waiting for the family to gather around it. Candlelight gleams on the silver, and tantalizing aromas rise from the serving dishes. There is thick gravy on the roast; lots of butter and cream in the mashed potatoes. Buttered corn and creamed carrots. Rolls. The dessert stands on the sideboard—a delectable seven layer Viennese torte mounded with whipped cream. How tempting! How beautiful! But wait. All is not what it seems. There is distortion here. Strokes, heart attacks, high blood pressure, circulatory disorders, and even death hides here for the family that eats this way. Yet this same attractively appointed table, by presenting delicious *good* foods, can hold slimness, health, and even life for the family that dines at it. Think!

Dinner, Meal #3, is the pinnacle of the eating day. After the long afternoon span, this is the meal at which we relax and refresh ourselves from the day's activities. It is most important, then, that Meal #3 be attractively prepared and served, so that it is pleasing to the eye as well as to the palate. Meal #3, like the other two daily meals, should always be varied, from meal to meal and from day to day. Variation of protein is the first thing to be considered. Protein is meat, fish, poultry, egg, cheese— usually the main course at any meal. To illustrate: if egg has been consumed at Meal #1, and fish has been the Meal #2 choice, then beef may be served at Meal #3. That day's variation pattern of protein has then been egg, fish, beef. If the previous day's pattern has been, for example, poultry, cheese, and veal at the three successive meals, then you have two days of perfect variation, and that variation is important for fastest weight loss, as well as for balanced food intake.

One word of caution: beef, the most popular of American meats, is, unfortunately, rather high in caloric value, and so beef meals should be widely spaced. Be careful that you do not find yourself constantly eating beef in one form or another. Two or three beef dinners each week are permissible, with three or four beef breakfasts and/or lunches, as a lesser quantity is consumed at those meals. Although beef may be eaten each day, you may not have it for the same meal each day or for successive meals in any one given day.

We suggest that the following meats be avoided completely:

Tongue (very high in calories)

Pot Roast (Cooks in own fat juices)

All pork products (high fat content, high in calories) These three meat items may be indulged in, if desired, after excess weight is lost. The avoidance is only temporary while proceeding toward your weight goal.

At Meal #3, vegetables should also be varied. Don't be rigid about vegetables. That's fat thinking. Try some unfamiliar vegetables. They are real friends to the weight loser. They provide the bulk that keeps you feeling satisfied, and they are smart substitutes for enemy foods. By varying all your vegetables, you inadvertently balance off calorie intake and also supply yourself with all of the vitamins and minerals you need. Keep attractiveness in mind, and remember how colorful the yellow, orange, and green vegetables can be when served in clever artistic combinations. For example, the bright orange of whole baby carrots served with brilliant green leaf spinach!

To keep yourself interested, vary your salads, too. Salad does not simply have to be a boring bowl of crumpled lettuce. Consult the Salad Section in the Recipe pages for attractive, eye-and-taste-appealing salad ideas.

Cheese and eggs are unwise choices for Meal #3. This is mainly because the fat content of these two items being what it is, they would have to be consumed in much smaller quantities than meat, fish, or poultry can be, leaving the diner probably unsatisfied. Lack of satisfaction of hunger at Meal #3 can be dangerous. It frequently leads to unselective, unwise refrigerator raiding later in the evening. Most overweight people have the habit of evening snacking combined with a compulsion to eat enemy foods. If a skimpy Meal #3 is added to this combination, the would-be reducer finds it far too easy to succumb to temptation.

Let us return to our image of the attractive family dinner table. American families often have notoriously poor eating habits, consuming far too many foods high in saturated fats, starches, and sugars. While you are personally concerned with yourself in the areas of food, eating, and weight loss, it is most desirable and beneficial to introduce your entire family, if possible, to balanced, healthful eating. Why not? It is totally unnecessary to prepare meals differently for yourself and thus spend extra hours in the kitchen. For example, if roast lamb

49

is the meat planned for the family dinner, include Think Thin items with it, such as a Think Thin soup to start, at least two hot vegetables interestingly prepared, and a tempting salad. Then add baked potatoes, or rice, or noodles for the slim members of the family, although you yourself will naturally abstain from these. Good eating habits should ideally begin in childhood and can prevent heart disease, arteriosclerosis, and overweight in later life. If you can gradually convert your entire family to balanced, healthful eating, your weight loss project can be a boon to all of them.

When you have rounded off your nutritional day by consuming a full and satisfying Meal #3, you will find yourself well-equipped to get through the evening hours with comfort. Persons attempting to lose weight by "cutting down" on their three daily meals or by skipping some of them entirely often wind up doing "enemy" cheating at night. Because of your three satisfying, properly balanced meals and your consequent high nutritional level, you have a good chance of being satisfied with the non-detrimental snacks we recommend, such as Chiffon Gelatin, fresh fruits, milk shakes, etc.*

* See Recipe Section and Chapter 8.

7. RETRAINING YOUR TASTES

To become slim and to remain slim, you must enlist your body chemistry as an ally. We have found, from personal experience and from working with thousands of overweight persons, that if enemy foods are abstained from for a period of generally not less than five weeks and rarely more than seven weeks, the appetite adjusts, the body chemistry adjusts, and the craving or desire for high fat or high carbohydrate items subsides and often vanishes. In the few cases where it does not disappear entirely, it becomes so insignificant as to no longer be a factor of any importance.

To illustrate: If chocolate in its myriad forms is your particular hangup, and you are able to abstain from it (and abstain means to do *entirely* without), somewhere within the span of five to seven weeks, depending on the individual, you really will lose your terrible craving for chocolate. If, however, you consume even one square of a chocolate bar, one tiny wedge of chocolate cake, or one small brownie, you reset your body chemistry for chocolate and you must then start the whole routine of abstinence over again. In the beginning, it might seem quite difficult to abstain—to substitute something allowable for the desired chocolate or sometimes to just have to say a firm "no" to chocolate, but in the long run it

51

is the easiest and the only way to permanent slimness.

Substituting something allowable during the period of abstinence can sometimes involve vegetables, and, of course, few fat people really like vegetables in any form. Some of the greatest fat rigidity concerns vegetables. If dieting fat persons go to parties, they can be frighteningly flexible when urged to indulge in forbidden fruits. Slim Sara says to overweight Mildred:

"Oh, Millie, you've been dieting for years! What difference will one more day make. Go on, take a piece of cake!"

Or Jack, who has never had a weight problem and just doesn't understand, urges fat Harry:

"Harry, my wife made that baked macaroni and cheese just for you. Go ahead, have some. Start the damned diet tomorrow!"

How pathetically easy it is for fat people to succumb to these suggestions! But if an unfamiliar, or even a familiar, vegetable is offered or suggested, their flexibility quickly reverts to rigidity again. They refuse adamantly. They just can't stand vegetables. Period.

Most fat people are inclined to be rigid about their eating habits. They like only what they like, and that's that. And, sadly, they more than "like." They say, with expressions of near-ecstasy:

"I *adore* potato pancakes!"

"I'm *crazy* for pizza!"

"I *love* hot fundge sundaes!"

What they fail to understand is that food of any kind does not really merit love. Normally slim people "prefer," "like," or "enjoy" certain foods (usually salads, vegetables, fruits, meats, and so on), but they usually do not claim to "love" them. Food is not all that important to them, and so their eating remains in the proper perspective. This is not to imply that all slim people are paragons of virtue in their eating, but in the final analysis, they do not eat more than their bodies can burn up, and so they remain slim. Overweight "lovers" of potato pancakes and hot fudge sundaes would do better to save that misguided love for spouses and children rather than wasting it on food, and enemy food at that.

Unfortunately, the enemy foods that overweight people "love" are keeping them fat and making them fatter. For years they have been priming their bodies with high fat and high carbohydrate junk foods. Consequently, their appetites demand more and more of these junk foods, sometimes to the exclusion of almost every other edible, and a vicious circle continues itself. The more junk they eat, the fatter they get, the less they do, the fatter they get, and so on, ad infinitum.

For the overweight person who *really* wants to be slim, the importance of making an effort to overcome this rigidity cannot be stressed strongly enough. You can at least *try* to learn to like a few vegetables. Vegetables are great friends that help valiantly to fight the high fat and high carbohydrate enemies. Substituted for french fries, pizzas, gravies, cakes, ice creams, and so forth, vegetables provide bulk and a feeling of fullness. Vegetables can even make you feel righteous, in a sense. When you want sincerely to lose weight and you try a few vegetables, you often begin to feel that you are doing something right for a change!

The stomach has no brains. It is content to be filled with almost anything at all, and it's not in the least particular. It is the brain, controlling the appetite, that

53

dictates what to eat to satisfy. And if your brain is accustomed to choosing junk foods, soon only junk signals to the brain that you are satisfied. With a little
forethought, this can be changed. A stomach filled with
a peck of spinach feels just as replete as a stomach filled
with chocolate cake. Keeping your stomach full and
satisfied with vegetable friends is a big help in fighting
the temptation to cheat with enemy foods. This takes
conscious effort, because you're just not going to want
to do that. Fat people tell themselves that by skimping
on meals they'll lose more weight, when all they are
really doing is trying to give themselves leeway to cheat.

There are other benefits to be derived from learning
to like vegetables. Many of the green and leafy vegetables
are natural diuretics, which help drive fluids through
the body mechanism and so contribute to weight loss.
Furthermore, many overweight persons are happily
surprised to discover how good plain vegetables can
taste without the adornment of cream sauces or butter
sauces. The wonderful natural flavors come through
when vegetables are prepared without high calorie trim-
mings and additives. And there's another bonus. If you
eat lots of vegetables and vary them continually from
day to day, you will inadvertently ingest most of the
vitamins and minerals your body needs for maximum
nutrition and good health, which leads to vigor, vitality,
and much less fatigue.

So if you really want to be slim badly enough, give
yourself a fighting chance and enlist vegetables as one of
your aids in winning the battle of overweight. Get re-
acquainted with some of the vegetables you already know
about. Try some unfamiliar ones. There *are* other vegetables besides peas and carrots and string beans, you

know! How about a Garlic Artichoke? Or Baked*
Zucchini? Or Broccoli Espagnole? The recipes are all
to be found in the Recipe Section under the heading:
Vegetables. Get to know some of them. You'll be glad
you did!

Try not to think rigidly about salads, either. Salad
does not have to be just some dull, boring, torn-up
lettuce. That's the way fat people think! Easy, attractive salads can be invaluable for padding out meals
and as between meal snacks, and that's the way slim
people think! Reverse your attitude and start thinking
thin. Consult the Recipe Section under the heading:
Salads, and use your imagination!

For best results, remember that your three daily meals
should include satisfying amounts of protein (meat,
fish, poultry, eggs, cheese). Many overweight people
say,

"But I just don't like meat!"

This is another sample of rigid fat thinking. Yet
protein is the most important food category of all. Protein satisfies hunger the best and burns fat the best. If
you are really thinking thin, you'll make the small
effort involved in determining the amounts of protein
that satisfy *you*. Consult the Recipe Section for attractive, easy-to-prepare, varied protein recipes. Meat courses
do not have to be plain old steak, roast beef, and broiled
chicken only. Keep yourself interested and prevent
eating-boredom and possible subsequent cheating with
enemy foods. Try the Chili recipe. Or Stuffed Peppers.
Or Veal Rolls. Attempt to expand your "likes."

While too much protein is also stored as fat, we believe it is preferable to have perhaps an extra small piece
of chicken which may help you fortify yourself against

satisfying appetite later with ice cream or cake. After all, very few, if any, fat people became fat because they ate too much meat!

Substituting allowable food for detrimental enemy items could be called the Think Thin Game. It's challenging and enjoyable to see how much good you can do yourself rather than harm, weight-wise, especially when it comes to sweets. While not all fat people are addictively attracted to sweets, a great proportion of them are. This is frequently caused by long-time conditioning, often from childhood. In many families with overweight members, sweets are usually the "reward" foods for the children.

"If you get a good report card, we'll buy you two dozen of those special barley-sugar lollipops."

"Poor baby! You've scraped your knee! Here's a cupcake to help you forget the sting."

And so it goes, until the conditioned reflex is formed —trouble, pain, reward, achievement—sweets make it feel better; sweets help celebrate. This is classic fat thinking, usually subconscious, and for the overweight person, it helps push eating even further out of perspective. In this way, sweets achieve a monumental importance for many of the overweight. Poor family eating patterns and traditional ethnic backgrounds can also contribute to this attitude.

However, permissible sweets can be substituted for non-permissible enemy sweets. If you want to lose weight and keep it off badly enough, face the fact that it is necessary to try to wean yourself away from the enemy sweet-eating habit. There is no room for sugar per se in an eating project designed by you for losing weight sensibly and permanently. But natural sugars, such as sucrose, glucose, lactose, etc., are lower in calories but are also satisfyingly sweet and are readily available in the form of fruit. Delicious fresh fruits in season can substitute for cakes, chocolates, candies and all the other forbidden sweets. In the Recipe Section under the heading: Fruit, some exciting ideas are offered for the preparation of tasty fruit dishes. Get the fruit habit. That's part of thinking thin! And think of all the vitamins and minerals!

Nor need you forego desserts entirely. Under the heading: Desserts, some delightful dessert suggestions can be found. They are colorful, taste-appealing, and low in calories. You will notice that a few of these dessert recipes involve artificially sweetened low-calorie sodas and sometimes small amounts of artificial sweeteners. This is a temporary solution to help fat people get over the hump of that craving for sweets. In their own personal weight-losing experiences, the authors found moderate amounts of artificial sweetners to be perfectly harmless to them.

However, because of the recent controversy over artificial sweeteners, the cyclamates in particular, we believe the use or non-use of these substances to be a highly individual matter. We therefore strongly suggest that each person consult a physician for a professional opinion as to the role artificial sweeteners may play in his individual project to lose weight.

We must point out that with the exception of low calorie sodas and moderate amounts of artificial sweetener in tea, coffee, or cooking, dietetic products as such do not belong in a project to lose weight permanently. Dietetic foods (those foods sweetened with chemical substances) were originally invented, not for the overweight, but for those persons, such as diabetics and sufferers from other conditions, who were *forced* to restrict their intake of ordinary sugars. As the percentage of overweight persons in this over-fed country of ours increased, Madison Avenue realized it was missing out on a good thing. Over eighty million Americans suffer from some kind of a weight problem today. So food company after food company climbed on the dietetic band wagon. Fat people, eager for any shortcut magic method for losing weight easily, provided a vast buying power for any and all dietetic products. Few of them lost any weight, and none of them lost permanently. What the overweight purchasers did not understand was that, in the main, the only difference in dietetic products is the substitution of artificial sweeteners for natural sugar. The starch was still there; the shortening was still there.

There is available on the market today dietetic cake, dietetic ice cream, and even dietetic chocolate. One manufacturer has gone to the fantastic extreme of brewing a dietetic beer! The sugar may be eliminated and the calories may be a bit lower than in a similar non-dietetic product, but it is still cake, still ice cream, still chocolate, and still beer. How is an overweight person, consuming these dietetic "goodies," going to be able to retrain his appetite and his thinking away from these enemy types of foods?* Dietetic chocolate tastes almost exactly like non-dietetic natural chocolate, and so the body chemistry will then continue to demand the taste of chocolate.

* *The authors do not consider cake, candy, ice cream, beer, and so forth to be "enemy" foods for slim people. Slim people know how to handle them. If you want to stay slim, you will have to learn how to handle them, too . . . and you will!*

Where does that leave you? Still with poor eating habits, still with the wrong kind of preferences, and, unfortunately, probably still fat!

Don't kid yourself. There is no magic short cut for losing weight permanently. In the long run, most dieting "short cuts" lead the dieter exactly nowhere. Learn to eat good foods instead of junk. Dietetic products are valuable medical substitutes when prescribed for those persons who really require them, but for weight losers, they are to be considered junk, even though they may be low in calories. So don't let yourself believe erroneously that dietetic products will help you lose weight and keep it off.

Thinking thin does not mean just losing weight. Thinking thin means learning to think like slim people think, and slim people think entirely differently about food and eating than overweight people do! Thinking thin means re-educating your appetite and your attitude—permanently.

8. THINK BEFORE YOU EAT

Overweight people, when they embark on a diet, (or on an eating project to lose weight permanently, as *we* prefer to call it), sometimes feel that they must withdraw from the world. They build figurative China walls around themselves. They hesitate to read or watch television because these activities trigger an eating association for them. They become fearful about snacking between meals. Maybe they'll go too far. They grow afraid to go out to a restaurant or to a friend's home. Perhaps they will be confronted with too many temptations.

But this is unnecessary negative thinking. There's no need to manufacture an artificial environment in which you cannot expect to exist very long anyhow. In this country, we live in a food-oriented society. There is a pizza parlor or an ice cream shop on almost every corner. Billboards urge the consumer to eat, eat, eat. Airline advertising, instead of emphasizing safety records or frequent flight schedules, stresses the foods that will be offered in flight.

"The best roast beef sandwich in the air!"

"Take our delicatessen flight to Chicago!"

"The finest wine cellar in the air!"

And what about the endless food commercials on television? No wonder TV watching often sends defeated dieters to their refrigerators! The point is that this emphasis on foods, and far too frequently junk foods at that, will always be there, and sooner or later, you will be forced to face the temptations. You really can learn to live with it if you will make the attempt to analyze and understand yourself, which leads to the ability to handle the whole problem.

You *can* read, you *can* watch television, and you *can* snack at those times without destroying what you are trying to accomplish with your weight. The first point to understand is that this kind of evening snacking is really compulsive eating. Compulsive eaters, which many fat people are, eat when they are not even hungry. Nibbling while you are reading or traveling to the refrigerator during TV commercials is not done because you are actually hungry. You are answering the dictates of appetite. Few overweight persons comprehend the difference between hunger and appetite. Hunger is a genuine instinct. When the body requires fuel to maintain energy, repair tissues, and sustain life, we feel *hunger*. But appetite is a learned reaction, a conditioned reflex. Appetite for snacks of peanuts, pretzels, candy, and so on, satisfies an emotional need rather than a physical one. Appetite makes us eat when we are not really hungry at all.

If you are a compulsive eater pushed around by your appetite, you probably always will be. Yet this really does not necessarily present an insurmountable problem when you are involved in an eating project to lose weight permanently. Compulsive eaters can go right on being compulsive if they take the time and trouble to think first. Remember, it's not how much you eat, it's *what* you eat that counts. Snacking in between is perfectly permissible if you can learn to be *selective*. Most intelligent people are selective about their clothes, selective about their hairdos, selective about their friends, selective about education for their children, etc. Carry this selectivity one step further. Eating is one of the most important things we do, as we *are* what we eat, in a sense. How equally important, then, to be selective about what we eat.

For example: You have settled down for an evening of television. After an hour or so, you feel that old familiar urge to nibble on something. But you are trying very hard to lose weight! What to do? It's simple. Start thinking.

The section of this book called "Think Thin Menus" lists Food Categories. Under Item #5, Vegetables, there is a list headed B. All of the vegetables in List B can be eaten in absolutely unlimited quantities because they have so little significant calorie value. Guided by this list, why not prepare a television "Treat Tray"—a sort of antipasto of crisp, fresh vegetables? Vary the textures, the tastes, and the colors, so that both the eye and the palate will be intrigued. Here is a sample "Treat Tray":

Dill pickle strips
Raw cauliflower buds
Radish roses
Green pepper rings
Squares of red pimiento
Celery sticks
Cucumber circles

Or, of course, any combination of B items that you prefer. Sprinkle with salt and pepper, and, if you desire, a dash of wine vinegar or fresh lemon juice, or an envelope of bouillon powder for seasoning, and you will find your fingers and your mouth well occupied for quite a while.

Prefer something sweet? That's no problem, either.

Men are allowed five servings of fruit each day, and women are allowed three servings. (This is an optional item, not a necessity.) If you know you are an habituated TV snacker, do not consume all of your fruit allowance during the day. Save one or two or all of them for TV time. A crisp delicious red apple. A juicy fresh peach. Half a canteloupe. And don't eat the tiniest piece of fruit you can find, either. Select the largest pieces available. Even a gigantic Cortland apple has fewer calories than even a teeny wedge of chocolate cake!

If you desire something a bit more exotic, check the Fruit category in the Recipe Section. Pineapple Ambrosia is deliciously sweet. Apple or Fruit Pie, Think Thin style, can make you feel as if you are eating something delightfully illegal! And what about trying a Blue and Gold Surprise?

Of course, fruit is limited since men are confined to five servings and women are confined to three. If you really are terribly compulsive during an evening, you might also try one of the unlimited desserts. Unlimited means exactly that. You may actually consume all you want without detriment to your eating project. In the Desserts category, there are several delicious unlimiteds. Orange Chiffon appeals to everyone. Or try Jello Jems, Coffee Gel, or Fresh Lemon Gelatin.

You're not overly fond of skim milk? For good, balanced nutrition, all adults, whether they are following diets to lose weight or not, should consume a pint of milk each and every day, preferably skim milk, and this is especially important for dieters in connection with retention of skin tone while losing weight, particularly if you have a good deal of weight to lose. Balanced nutrition, including skim milk, helps prevent the sagging,

baggy, tired look that afflicts unwise dieters. If you find
it a hardship to *drink* your daily required pint of skim
milk, you can *eat* your milk allotment instead, and at
the same time provide yourself with a tasty reading or
television snack. The Dessert recipe for Custard Treat
uses the entire day's milk allowance and fills four custard cups. Line up the custard cups and treat yourself!
Other recipes that involve the skim milk allowance are:

"Carvel" Think Thin style

Tangy Orange Mold

Orange Sherbet

Pineapple Sherbet

Strawberry Sherbet

And, of course, if you like drinking the skim milk but
would enjoy it more dressed up a little, we suggest a
Milk Shake or an Egg Cream. You'll really enjoy both.
Check the Index for recipes.

There will be moments, especially at the start of your
new eating project, when, no matter how hard you think
or how intelligently selective you try to be, your bad-
habit-oriented appetite will scream for candy, chocolate
cookies, ice cream, or whatever, until your body chemistry
adjusts during the period of abstinence. At those particular difficult moments, no substitute will do, no kind
of selectivity seems to help. Then ask yourself:

"Right now, does my motivation to be slim outweigh
my desire for this enemy food?"

If you can honestly say "Yes, it does," we suggest that
it might be helpful at this moment to change your activity pattern for a short while. Get up out of your chair
and take a short walk. Not a mile-long hike, but perhaps just a slow stroll around your block. This can do
a lot for your mental attitude, too. You are altering a

poor leisure habit. Instead of merely sitting and doing nothing, as overweight people are prone to do, you are at least doing *something*. This little stroll can help divert your attention from your clamoring appetite. Or telephone a friend and spend a few minutes in pleasant conversation.

Sometimes, when all else fails, though, you'll just have to say a firm "No!" to your appetite. If you can do this, you'll be surprised at the uplift your confidence in your own abilities receives. You'll feel proud of yourself! And pride in self is one of the classic benefits of becoming slim.

What about that empty feeling that seems to afflict so many people in the late afternoon? Doctors say that this may be caused by a drop in blood sugar levels, so it is a legitimate physical feeling. It's a mistake to just try to ignore the sensation. Gritting your teeth and hanging on when you feel a need to eat something is rarely a sensible thing to do. That soon becomes uncomfortable, and to see an eating project through to its successful completion, you should attempt at all times to keep yourself feeling comfortable and relaxed. The solution is, of course, to eat or drink something allowable at once.

In cold weather, there's nothing better for that four o'clock feeling than a mug of steaming hot bouillon. Several companies make excellent beef, chicken, vegetable, or onion bouillon cubes or powders. The powders are perhaps simpler and quicker to use, as they dissolve immediately. All you do is add hot water. If plain bouillon fails to satisfy sufficiently, add vegetables to it, according to some of the unlimited recipes in the Recipe Section under the heading: Soups. In their own personal successful weight-losing projects, the authors often made up large quantities of dishes such as Mushroom Soup, Cabbage Soup, Vegetable Bouillon, and Bean Sprout Soup, and kept them on hand in covered containers in their respective refrigerators. This was their ammunition to help fight late afternoon eating indiscretions. If you permit yourself to become hungry enough, and there is nothing allowable available, intelligence and selectivity fly out the window, and you're likely to eat anything at all. So be prepared!

A glass of iced low calorie soda, in warm weather, is a valuable late afternoon aid. Or again, a Milk Shake, or a Think Thin Egg Cream. Be sure, of course, to have the necessary ingredients for these items on hand at all times. That's important. If there is nothing there but a pecan coffee ring, that's probably what you'll eat!

If you employ your intelligence, there is absolutely no need to be frightened by the challenge of eating in a restaurant when you are following an eating project to lose weight. Many successful dieters have eaten the major proportion of their daily meals in restaurants through sheer necessity in their particular life styles. Dining out does not have to be a problem, either to the constant restaurant diner or to the occasional social restaurant visitor.

If dinner or luncheon in a restaurant is scheduled to take place later than your usual time for consuming those meals, the wisest maneuver is to fortify yourself first, if possible just before leaving your home. Take the edge off that hungry feeling by having a Think Thin Baked Apple and a cup or two of coffee; or a fruit Milk Shake; or perhaps a good-sized bowl of Orange Chiffon. This principle of fortifying yourself first can increase your selectivity abilities when confronted with an exotic restaurant menu. Once again, the old rule about being too hungry applies. If you fail to fortify yourself first, hunger and appetite combined can cause you to order anything and everything without thinking. Taking the edge off is really a method of supplying yourself with will power and the ability to select intelligently foods that will not destroy all your good efforts at weight-losing and re-educating your appetite.

Having fortified yourself first, read down the menu. Do you want an appetizer first? Perfectly allowable, if you select a shrimp, lobster, or crabmeat cocktail, a fresh fruit cup, tomato juice, or something similar. Then you will discover that almost every good restaurant serves roast beef, steak, turkey, lobster, shrimp, chicken, and so forth. These are all permissible items. Some kind of salad usually accompanies every restaurant meal. Ask that yours be served without dressing, and request vinegar or lemon wedges brought with it. Insist that your vegetables be served to you without butter or cream sauces, and be sure to order at least two. The dessert hurdle? No hurdle at all. Select fresh fruit if they have it, or just have a second cup of tea while the others in your party have their dessert. If the others are slim, desserts are certainly allowable for them. If the others are overweight, they shouldn't be eating gooey desserts, either, and if they do, you can sit there and feel superior!

After all of this, you'll feel replete and satisfied. More important, you'll have a definite respect for yourself, rather like a warrior returning victorious from a major decisive battle! For once you used your brain and didn't just sit there gorging yourself on idiotic, unnecessary high-calorie "goodies" like an eating machine!

One word of caution: it might be wise, temporarily,

to avoid Chinese and Italian restaurants. After all, fat people do not visit these two types of eating establishments with the idea of eating properly. They go to a Chinese restaurant with egg rolls and roast pork in mind, and to Italian restaurants to consume spaghetti. These, obviously, are enemy foods for weight-losers!

So go ahead out to eat and enjoy yourself. Dinner out in a restaurant should not signify food alone. Dining out for social or business reasons means, to slim people, stimulating conversation and enjoyable companionship. Start thinking that way. Break down that mythical China wall!

Many fat people find that for them the toughest situation of all is to be invited to a meal at the home of a friend. What on earth can you do when your hostess insists that she prepared the macaroni casserole especially with you in mind? Naturally, the prime function of a hostess is to please her guests. If you've been overweight for some time, she suspects, with truth, that rich foods are the quickest way to your heart, and so that is what she will offer you. How can you avoid embarrassing either yourself or your hostess?

When you come right down to it, it is certainly much more embarrassing to be fat than to politely refuse a proffered dish, but if this kind of basic thinking doesn't help you, perhaps this can. With so many people following diets of one kind or another these days, a new set of social rules is in force. It is perfectly correct for a guest to say, "No, thank you," and it is considered gauche and graceless of a hostess to insist in the face of this polite refusal. After all, she would not press a richly sugared dessert on a person she knows to be severely diabetic, nor would she attempt to force an alcoholic beverage on a guest who is a confessed member of Alcoholics Anonymous. Obesity is also a disease, and you must think of yourself as being just as disabled, so to speak, as the diabetic or the alcoholic, and continue to refuse.

The rules are: Fortify yourself first at home; accept what is allowable for you; graciously refuse what you are not permitted to have. This isn't always easy, but in the long run, it's worth it! In the event that you know your hostess very well, you might also quietly bring along something you *can* have, if you discover ahead of time that dishes unwise for you will be served. If this is impossible, plan on following the above rules. You can always have something proper for you at home later.

In any eventuality, a real problem can exist only if you want it to. This applies to every situation where eating is involved, business, social, or just the daily round of which your particular life style consists. If your motivation to be slim is strong enough, you'll be able to handle anything that comes along.

9. COPING WITH SOCIAL OCCASIONS

Long ago in our American culture, when people often lived at great distances from each other, social get-togethers had different significance from what they do today. A wedding, a christening, or a barn-raising provided a unique opportunity for friends and neighbors to gather together for conversation, gossip, square-dancing, mutual endeavor and intellectual exchange. Refreshments were important, but somehow they were always secondary. In the struggle to settle and build a nation, first things came first. Because people were concentrating on survival, gourmet goodies were seldom available, although good plain food was. Nevertheless, mutual effort and friendship and good neighborliness mattered far more than eating.

Holidays such as Thanksgiving and Christmas specifically meant the gathering of family from far and wide. Naturally a feast was prepared, but it most assuredly was not the be-all, end-all of the occasion. Today, however, life is different. We are softer, and we have more, much more, especially food. Eating has assumed a significance far out of proportion to its basic meaning. Weddings, christenings, Bar Mitzvahs, and holidays seem to make a focal point out of the repast to be served, particularly to the overweight. How many hostesses today plan their menus before they even consider their guest lists!

Most normally slim people are still able to keep eating in its proper perspective, but with a greater percentage of the American population overweight all the time, social emphasis shifts more and more to food. Even the American tradition of the annual vacation is affected. Mention the word "cruise" to slim people, and nine chances out of ten, their eyes will light up as they discuss the dances, the swimming pool, the shuffle board, and the exotic ports of call they will visit. Fat persons, on the other hand, will describe at ecstatic length the beauties of the daily luncheon smörgasbord and the gourmet dinners served each night aboard ship. This is the first aspect of the cruise that comes to their minds. And so it is apparent that vacations, holidays, and social occasions signify quite different things to the slim and to the overweight.

Overweight people who are engaged in eating projects to lose weight consequently are concerned and even fearful about entertaining at social functions or holidays. Take that great traditional American holiday, Thanksgiving, for instance. How are you to provide the expected feast for family and friends, pleasing them, but not subjecting yourself to undue temptations that might jeopardize your efforts with your good eating project? The key, once again of course, is *thinking*. A colorful, attractive, and delicious Thanksgiving dinner can be served according to the following suggested Think Thin menu. Slim guests or family members will enjoy it thoroughly. It's the kind of food they really prefer, anyhow. Overweight guests will enjoy it equally, and may never suspect that they are consuming one meal

72

that will not pad their fat bodies with additional unneeded calories! You can relax and enjoy your guests and the occasion, knowing that the feast is, in all respects, correct for you.

SUGGESTED THINK THIN THANKSGIVING MENU

(*Note:* Recipes for starred items will be found in the Recipe Section. See Index for page numbers.)

Shrimp cocktail
Roast turkey with Think Thin stuffing*
Cranberry Relish*
Relish dish (radish roses, scallions, green pepper rings)
Tossed salad
Stuffed hearts of celery
    (Stuff with mixture of blue and cottage cheeses)
Mashed turnips
French-style string beans
Broccoli stalks
Chiffon Pumpkin Pie*
Coffee or tea

(*Note:* For slim guests or family members, you may add creamed onions and some form of potatoes, if desired.)

Christmas is another traditional holiday that need present no real problem. Exchange gifts with family and friends in remembrance of Christ's birthday. Don't focus on food. The three kings from the East brought to the infant Jesus gold, frankincense, and myhrr, not cream pies or pizzas! Get out your best china and linens and trim your Christmas table with holly and colored ornaments and tall red candles. Then prepare and serve the following delightful Think Thin Christmas dinner:

73

SUGGESTED THINK THIN
CHRISTMAS DINNER MENU

(*Note:* If you truly want to be slim, we suggest that you confine your cup of Christmas Cheer to some kind of non-alcoholic beverage. Feel free to serve cocktails or eggnogs to slim guests and those not on diets, but without calling attention to the fact, serve yourself a Horse's Neck* or a Think Thin Cocktail*).

(*Note:* Starred items will be found in the Recipe Section. See Index for page numbers.)

Chopped Chicken Liver appetizer*
Rib Roast of Beef
Pickled Bean Salad*
Relish dish (radish roses, scallions, green pepper rings)
Lettuce, tomato, and cucumber salad
Baked Acorn Squash*
  (Tastes almost exactly like sweet potatoes)
Asparagus spears with pimiento strips
Think Thin Mashed Potatoes*
Rainbow Dessert*
Coffee or tea

* * *

Two holidays in which the emphasis has shifted much too far away from the original meanings are Easter, for Christian people, and Passover, for Jewish people. Many would-be weight losers fall down badly on Easter or Passover.

Chocolate bunnies, jelly eggs, and Easter hams have nothing whatever to do with the Resurrection of Christ, particularly ham. Christ himself was a Jew, to whom pork was forbidden by the dietary laws, so it is a purely recent traditional invention. No precept of the Christian religion calls for the consumption of ham at Easter time, or for any other specific food for that matter. Lent, in fact, points exactly the other way. Lent commemorates Christ's forty days of fasting and soul searching in the desert, and Christian attention should ideally be directed away from food during the Lenten period. As pork products are a poor idea for anyone who sincerely wishes to lose weight, why not serve an Easter turkey or an Easter capon or Easter lamb?

Matzoh ball soup and fancy Passover cakes are not a religious requirement for Jewish people during the festival of Passover, either. True, certain dishes, such as the bitter herbs and charoset do have religious meaning, but surely they can merely be symbolically tasted rather than devoured gluttonously! Many Jewish dieters worry unnecessarily about the traditional four glasses of wine that are served at Passover Seders. Again, a symbolical sip will fulfill your religious obligation satisfactorily. Oddly enough, many contemporary Jews have only the vaguest idea of what the four glasses signify, anyway. Murray J. Siegel, a Jew himself, states: "If you know *exactly* what each glass of wine represents religiously, you may go ahead and drink them!"

During Passover, matzoh can be substituted for the daily white bread allotment required in your eating project. One half a matzoh will be approximately equivalent to one slice of regular enriched white bread, for the *Passover period only*.

To the authors, it is a rather sad commentary on contemporary life that the religious significance of many of our holidays has become submerged in and obscured by the feasting connected with them. Christmas, Easter, Passover, and even Thanksgiving are basically religious occasions, or should be, and not merely opportunities for the overweight to gorge themselves further! You will find it helpful in your eating project to focus your attention on the true basic meanings of all the holidays you celebrate. That's another part of Thinking Thin.

A point of interest, while we are discussing religion, is that the Bible refers to the self indulgence of overeating as the sin of gluttony. Most other sins or transgressions are known only to the sinners who commit them, but the sin of gluttony is one that a fat body advertises openly to one and all! This is a point to ponder if you consider yourself a truly religious person!

Like holidays, purely social dinner parties can be given without undue worry about the role eating will play for you personally during the occasion. You will find the following suggested Think Thin Dinner Party Menu most helpful in planning your entertaining when you are observing an eating project to lose weight:

SUGGESTED THINK THIN
DINNER PARTY MENU

(*Note:* If you serve cocktails before dinner, remember to provide for yourself a non-alcoholic allowable beverage as suggested in the Beverage section. If you wish to serve cocktail tidbits such as potato chips and pretzels to guests, do so, but be sure to include an attractive platter of cut-up colorful raw vegetables for yourself, accompanied by a dip made from cottage cheese flavored with minced onion and seasonings. You may be surprised to find your guests dipping into this!)

(*Note:* Starred items will be found in the Recipe Section. See Index for page numbers.)

Crabmeat cocktail
Mushroom Soup*
Roast Leg of Lamb
Minted Carrots*
Broccoli Espagnole*
Think Thin Mashed Potatoes*
Perfection Salad*
Hearts of celery and cucumber sticks
Jewel Parfaits*
Coffee or tea

When you are the recipient of an invitation to a large social function such as a wedding, a Bar Mitzvah, or a party of some kind, the rules for dining in restaurants or at the home of friends can still assist you. Always be sure to fortify yourself first, just before leaving your home. Face the fact that social drinking of alcoholic beverages is temporarily not for you, if you have a sincere desire to be slim, and plan to quietly request club soda on the rocks or a Bloody Mary without the Mary. (Plain tomato juice). As long as you hold a glass in your hand, you will find that comments will be few or nonexistent. No one really cares, anyway. You only think they do! Be as selective as possible with whatever is being served, avoiding those dishes which are obviously not allowable on your eating project and serving yourself generously with those that are not detrimental. Remember that it is quite correct to say politely but firmly, "No, thank you," if the necessity arises.

This is independence in eating. And this independence is a goal all persons wishing to lose weight should strive to attain. *You* are the one who should dictate what you will eat or drink. Not your friends, not your family,

77

and not your hostess. Independence in eating must be preceded by independence in thinking. Both can be achieved if you keep working at understanding yourself and your own particular eating difficulties, through personal nutritional analysis.

Enjoy yourself at the party. Dance, chat, laugh, exchange ideas. You have a secret weapon. And that secret weapon is you yourself and your deep motivation to lick your weight problem once and for all. Think of the wonderful opportunities you are going to have to shine at social gatherings when you have become slim!

Stop worrying about how to handle your eating when and if you are going on a vacation, whether it is to be a short trip or an extended journey. All that is required is a bit of thinking ahead. If you plan to travel by automobile, a most intelligent investment is a small, inexpensive styrofoam ice chest with a tight-fitting cover. Keep it in the back seat or trunk of your car, filled with ice cubes. The following items should be stored in it, as your personal ammunition against making serious eating errors, just in case you find yourself confronted with a situation where nothing proper is available:

THINK THIN TRAVELER'S SURVIVAL KIT

Fresh fruit (apples, pears, oranges, etc.)
Cans of low-calorie soda
Jar of dill pickles
Pound of chicken roll from your delicatessen
Few slices of cheese
Small loaf of white bread

Or, of course, whatever your personal preferences might be of allowable items. This kind of "be prepared" thinking has saved the day for the authors more than once! This is specifically "thinking thin."

If you are traveling by plane, train, etc., to a specific location, be sure to carry a handbag or a briefcase large enough to hold a few pieces of fresh fruit for those times when hunger or appetite strike without warning. A few envelopes of bouillon powder stowed away in a pocket are an additional insurance policy against eating incorrectly. When you reach your final destination, understand that even in foreign countries there are food stores of some kind where at least some proper foods can be obtained. Spend a few minutes on your first day there to purchase allowable or unlimited items which you will keep in your hotel room to fortify yourself first, or just in case of eating emergency.

Concentrate on the sight-seeing and activity aspects of your vacation and don't worry too much about the eating aspects. Think first, of course, but don't dwell on it. That's putting eating back into its proper perspective for vacations and trips. And have a wonderful time!

10. YOU AND YOUR FAMILY

Many fat people who fall from grace and commit eating indiscretions against the rules of their planned eating projects try to blame their failures on their children. They explain that the cookie jar was full of chocolate chip cookies, and the cupboards bulged with cupcakes, pretzels, potato chips, and other assorted junk foods because they had been purchased with the children in mind. And, inevitably, because the temporarily forbidden junk foods were so easily accessible to them right in their own cupboards and refrigerators, the temptation became too much for them and they succumbed. Then they say belligerently:

"But I don't want to deprive my kids!"

This kind of attitude is one of the reasons why the American people get fatter all the time. It is true that many slim youngsters seem to eat junk foods almost exclusively without apparently developing weight problems. But eventually, because of long term unbalanced poor eating habits, a frightening proportion of these kids wind up as overweight adults unless they are very lucky and happen to possess extremely active metabolisms and a great deal of nervous energy.

Why depend on luck with *your* family? You can gradually introduce your entire family to proper healthful eating habits at the same time you are engaged in losing weight and correcting your own poor attitudes about food. The newest concept, according to the opinion of the American Medical Association, is that the best cure for obesity is prevention. The medical profession apparently feels that almost all obese adults are hopeless incurables. While we most emphatically disagree with *that* attitude, we must join the doctors enthusiastically in their statement about prevention.

The place to start is with children, the younger the better. A most interesting and significant research experiment was once carried out with eighteen-month-old youngsters in a home for orphaned children. Three times each day, trays of various kinds of foods were placed in the youngsters' dormitory, and they were allowed to eat whatever they chose without direction or suggestion. For two consecutive days, a particular child might eat only bananas. Then for three days, perhaps he selected only cereal. However, at the end of a month, it was determined that each child had eaten a diet perfectly balanced for his own specific body needs, apparently by sheer instinct. The conclusions drawn from this experiment indicate that young children, like wild animals, tend to eat only what their bodies really require. Most children, then, if left strictly alone, would doubtless develop nothing but good eating habits. It is the examples and pressures of parents, siblings, and the outside world that influence a child's eating habits away from the ideal.

Young children *can* be taught that fresh, wholesome foods are essential to good health and slimness. The family meals should be planned around lean meat, poultry, fish, eggs, milk, and cheese, with plenty of fresh fruits and vegetables. Calorie-loaded desserts and mashed potatoes with gravy are dishes that should appear infrequently, if at all. Certainly desserts can be served, but they should be kept as much as possible in the fresh fruit, gelatins, and simple pudding areas. Cakes and pies can appear occasionally, but the important word is just that—occasionally.

Snacking between meals for children? Perfectly permissible, but offer your youngster apples, pears, celery or carrot sticks, and so on. If you are a mother, your attitude about your own eating project can be a wonderful educational example. Say,

"Here is a shiny crisp red apple. Here is a cake. Mommie is going to have a shiny red apple. You may have what you want."

As children are natural imitators, the child will soon be selecting the proper foods. This kind of thing then becomes his concept of a between-meal treat, and believe it or not, he actually will develop a preference for the right things. This is, of course, the "secret" of the lucky people who are slim by accident. They really prefer these types of foods to candies, cakes, and pies because emotionally and physically, they have become accustomed to them. We eat because we are hungry, and that is sheer instinct. We must eat in order to live. But *what* we eat is dictated by habit and appetite, and those are learned reactions. A youngster's habits and appetite can be trained from infancy on, and while this may require some initial discipline, the benefits of health and slimness in later life will be more than adequate reward.

This discipline, by the way, is not so much discipline of the child, but discipline of the parent. The young child requires no discipline to accept fruit and vegetable snacks. He will quite naturally enjoy these if this is what is customarily offered. But the parent, due to his or her own training, probably does not view these types of foods as true treats or snacks and may have to adjust his or her own thinking. Then there are the outside pressures of friends and neighbors, who may infer that you are a mean parent if you deny your children "goodies." But the child will be confronted with outside pressures of his own soon enough, and it is up to his parents to equip him to handle them. When he reaches his teens, with allowance money in his pocket, he will be associating with contemporaries who most probably will have execrable eating habits. There are pizza parlors and greasy-hamburger stands everywhere, and most teenagers today, unfortunately, eat this kind of garbage in preference to a balanced food intake, to the point where government health authorities are genuinely concerned about the long range implications for the nation's health.

It is totally unnecessary to reward even slim children with "goodies." Goodies that are not really goodies, but a most insidious form of menace to good health and slim fitness. We prefer to call these types of foods "baddies!" A far better reward than food is a family trip to a museum, a good movie, or a session at the bowling alley. Family celebrations should be an opportunity for sharing and exchanging ideas and experiences, and not just an unnecessary Roman feast of gorging.

There is a further corollary, and that is the "too thin" child, who simply must be "fattened up." Parents should, of course, be guided by their physicians in the case of an underweight child, but all too often they have never even consulted a physician. The child sometimes appears too thin in contrast to his chubby contemporaries or overweight members of his own family, and every effort is made to "feed him up." The old cliché about a lean horse for a long race is definitely true. The medical profession agrees unanimously that fat people live shorter lives than thin people, and it is far preferable to be slightly underweight than even slightly overweight. As a matter of fact, the attempt to fatten up the thin child can boomerang to exactly that emphasis on food that is so detrimental, and one day, there is another obese individual.

Parents have a definite responsibility to their children. Certainly they should be good examples in moral and ethical behavior and in social conduct. But if we are not to become an entire nation of overweight fatsos, wise parents should also try to set an example in their eating habits. Be a good nutritional image. Teach your children to eat to live, not to live to eat. Prevent obesity before it has a chance to start!

So if you have children, and you are inclined to be of the "I don't want to deprive my children!" school, *think!* In the first place, many overweight parents who ostensibly purchase enemy goodies for their children are really subconsciously purchasing them for themselves. This is the most classic of fat copouts! They don't feel quite so guilty when they succumb to temptation if they can rationalize that since they were forced to have the junk foods on hand for the benefit of the children, how could they themselves be expected to resist! Secondly, when your eating project is sound and sensible, and not just the lettuce leaf and the spoonful of cottage cheese you thought was correct for dieting in the past, it is unnecessarily difficult and foolish to prepare two sets of daily meals—one for you according to your individual

85

eating project and another for your family, probably heavily freighted with fats and carbohydrates. Basically, the three daily meals can be the same for each and every member of the family, and *should be*. The dishes described in the Recipe Section are delicious and attractive and will appeal to young and old. Certainly, if you have slim children or a slim spouse, you can add baked potatoes or a macaroni casserole or an occasional fancy dessert for them, but the basic menu should be sensible and balanced. Stop thinking about "depriving" your children. That's nonsense! For kids, true deprivation is having a fat parent, who is unattractive and unable to participate!

Through losing weight and re-educating your attitude about eating, you are guaranteeing your children and your spouse the eventual priceless gift of a slim, attractive and energetic parent and marital partner. Why not at the same time give your family, especially your children, the most valuable gift of all—a lifetime concept of good eating habits?

Thinking thin, whether you live alone or with a family, begins with menu planning. This takes only a short time to do each week and is well worth the small effort required. Menu planning by overweight persons, if they bother to do it at all, usually starts with the listing of seven gooey desserts, one for each day of the week. This is the ridiculous focal point around which the balance of the meal is haphazardly thrown together as an afterthought. This is obviously thinking fat. Thinking thin means considering protein first of all when plotting out a week's good eating for yourself and your family. List seven meat, poultry, or fish dishes for Meal #3, aiming at complete variation.

SAMPLE PROTEIN SELECTIONS:

Monday .... Beef
Tuesday .... Lamb
Wednesday .... Chicken
Thursday .... Beef
Friday .... Fish
Saturday .... Veal
Sunday .... Turkey

Plan on purchasing sufficient meat, poultry, or fish for the size of your family, plus a bit extra for leftovers that you can use for Meals #1 and Meals #2. Beef, for example, may be eaten every day as long as it is always consumed at a different meal on succeeding days. This is because lesser quantities are called for at Meal #1 and Meal #2 than at Meal #3, so that by always having beef at differing daily meals, you do not risk consuming maximum quantities of beef and consequently maximum calories. For a complete illustration of this concept, see the Sample Menus Section under the suggestions for 21 Consecutive Days.

As much variation as possible in fruits, vegetables, beverages, and salad ingredients is also a good idea for maximum weight loss and maximum nutrition. Consider this fact of variation also in planning your week's menus.

Once the menu has been prepared, make a shopping list based on the food items called for on your menus. This also takes very little time. This list can be flexible, so that advantage can be taken of possible unexpected supermarket sales, but it should definitely be made. You cannot shop hit or miss for food and then expect to wind up with everything on hand for a week of bal-

87

anced good eating. Beware of your fat subconscious. A fat subconscious is lazy and often rebels at having to plan or think ahead, but intelligent planning will help keep your nutritional house in order. By plotting weekly menus and preparing marketing lists based on such menus, you will soon learn to get much more nutrition for your food dollar. If you doubt this, try playing the Think Thin Shopping Cart game.

Here's how you play it: Enter any supermarket on a busy shopping day such as Friday or Saturday and observe the loaded shopping carts in the lines at the checkout counters. By scrutinizing the contents of each cart, you will quickly develop the ability to predict whether a fat person or a slim person is wheeling that cart without even glancing at the person first. Why and how? Because overweight shoppers, male or female, invariably have their shopping carts stacked high with empty-caloried junk foods—coffee rings, gallons of ice cream, frozen cakes, bags of pretzels and potato chips, and so forth. The carts of slim shoppers may also contain a few junk items, but you will also spot a preponderance of the high nutrition foods—heads of lettuce, bags of oranges and apples, bunches of broccoli, and similar things. Try this game. If you are an observant and earnest think thinner, you'll soon become expert at it!

Food costs are high these days and seem to get higher all the time. Be a wise shopper! Don't throw hard-earned money away by selecting empty-caloried junk. Buy good nutrition instead. And how much easier it is to eat correctly when only good nutritious food is on hand in your home!

It is a mistake to shop for groceries just before luncheon or just before dinner. Somehow, when you are feeling hungry, junk foods mysteriously seem to find their way into your shopping cart. Shopping right after a good satisfying meal makes it easier to stick to your planned shopping list. According to a recent article, this idea can even save you money. Studies showed that persons who shop right after a meal spend, on the average, about $5.00 less than usual. Conversely, persons who shop when they have not eaten for four or five hours tend to spend $7.00 more than usual.

Another good idea is to include in your shopping list the necessary ingredients for preparing allowable and unlimited snack foods. Be sure to purchase bouillon cubes or powders, low-calorie sodas, unflavored gelatin, etc. Then, after you put your marketing away at home, immediately prepare Orange Chiffon,* Zippy Cole Slaw,* Baked Apples,* soups, and so on, and keep them on hand as your ammunition against eating foolishly if hunger or appetite should suddenly attack you. Be prepared. Surround yourself with nutritional friends. Thinking thin also means thinking ahead!

(* Note: Starred items will be found in the Recipe Section. See Index for page numbers.)

11. HOW TO MAINTAIN YOUR NEW LOWERED WEIGHT

You've reached the weight goal that you set for yourself? Congratulations! Now for the final and most important step—learning how to maintain your wonderful new slimness. To insure this, we suggest that you perform five weeks of self-supervised tailor-made individual maintenance. Plan to continue weighing yourself once a week, exactly duplicating weigh-in conditions as instructed previously. First carry out a final review of your Check List. Do you still easily remember any of the items you originally checked? If so, and if any of these are of significant importance to you at this time, it is a good idea to plan to begin your maintenance with these items.

Maintaining lower weight is a highly individual matter, depending on a large number of factors and influenced by the exact manner in which the weight was lost. Various combinations of the following factors are involved:

Age (younger people, on the average, lose faster than older people)

Height (taller people seem to lose faster than shorter)

Basic body chemistry (Placid, sedentary people lose more slowly than nervous-energy types)

Environment (familial, social, ethnic)

Occupational activity (physical work as opposed to mental work)

Degree of poor eating habits

Persons who have lost weight through an eating project such as we have suggested and are ready to begin their maintenance projects can be roughly classified into four categories:

1. Good achiever (male) (female)
2. Fair achiever (male) (female)
3. Poor achiever (male) (female)
4. Non-achiever (male) (female)

To determine which category fits you personally, you should refer to your Weight Record Chart. Note where you have made the notation "G.B." on your Chart. This notation indicates that you have deviated excessively from your planned eating project in a given week and were still able to lose weight, although you could have lost considerably more, had you not deviated. Your record of losses, gains, "stayed evens," and "G.B.s" can help you draw pertinent conclusions as to what degree of maintenance you may project. The quantities and extents of foods that you may now add to your basic eating project depends strongly on the way your excess poundage was lost. To help you determine your category, and before we give you specific instructions, we will illustrate exact examples of each of the foregoing categories through actual case histories. (Names have been changed to protect personal privacy.) All of these cases are examples of safe, conservative maintenance foods added and substituted by each of these people according to their own individual preferences. You will, of course, be formulating your own additions and substitutions, based on your own likes and dislikes, but the following case histories will provide a good rule of thumb. Then, by making use of your Check List reviews, your Weight Record Chart, and your new nutritional knowledge of yourself, you can determine into which group you fall and can proceed accordingly with your own self-supervised maintenance project, guided by the instructions at the end of this chapter.

Category 1: Good achiever, male:

Jack G., age thirty-five, married, lost forty-two pounds in exactly sixteen weeks, and during five weeks of supervised maintenance he lost an additional three pounds. This can definitely be classified as a good achievement. During the sixteen weeks of his eating project, he did not deviate from his planned menus, and his between-meal snacking consisted entirely of allowables and unlimiteds. His variation in all foods was superb, and his difficulties were non-existent. On maintenance, Jack G. learned by a process of careful weekly experimentation that he could handle a maximum one week's maintenance level as follows:

Additions to his basic eating project
1. 5 Scotch and water highballs
2. 3 medium baked potatoes with 1 tablespoon cottage cheese on each
3. 3 two-inch wedges of cake (any kind)
4. Occasionally more than the allotted 5 fruits per day
5. Occasionally more than 1 serving of limited vegetables (See List C in Food Categories in the Menus section)

93

Substitutions in his basic eating project

1. Pot roast, corned beef, and cold cuts in approximately one half the quantities he had been consuming of permitted proteins
2. Rye bread occasionally in place of white bread

These additions and substitutions took place during one week of his maintenance project. His basic three-meal-concept pattern remained exactly the same as it had been during the sixteen-week period in which he lost the weight. Continuing the correct basic eating pattern is essential to proper maintenance. Close adherence to your balanced, nutritional three daily meals gives you the leeway to add and substitute during maintenance.

Because Jack G. was an excellent student of himself and his eating problems, he is now able to say confidently, "I now know more about myself, nutritionally speaking, than any doctor, nutritionist, or specialist who has ever examined me." But more than that, Jack G. understands how many extras he can consume without significant weight gain. If, however, he should slip and exceed his maintenance, and gain a little, he knows exactly how he lost the forty-two pounds in the first place, and he is able to revert to his basic eating project before the gain amounts to more than two or three pounds. He then arrives quickly back at his desired weight level and may proceed with his maintenance again. By re-educating and rehabilitating his attitude about eating and by placing eating in its proper perspective, Jack G. has become an independent and selective individual where food is concerned.

The chances of a good achiever ever slipping back

into his prior poor eating habits are almost impossible. Since he has exercised so much intelligence in his eating project to lose weight, it is equitable to assume that his maintenance will follow a similar intelligent pattern.

Category 1: Good achiever, female:

(While there are exceptions to every rule, in general, the female's ability to lose weight is less than that of the male. On the average, women lose one half as much as men, although they eat one third less food on their eating projects. The reasons for this discrepancy are physiological, since female body chemistry is different. Most females, during the pre-menstrual week lose less, because of the usual retention of fluids at this time, but *they will not gain* if they are observing their eating projects properly. Some females also find that a lesser weight loss takes place during the post-menstrual week as well, but they *will not gain if they are observing their eating projects properly*. So do not allow pre- or post-menstrual conditions to serve as a female fat copout!)

Mrs. Evelyn P., age thirty-nine, and the mother of *eight* children, lost 28¼ pounds in eleven weeks, and during five weeks of supervised maintenance, she lost an additional five pounds. This is an excellent achievement for a female. She was able to resist succumbing to the eating pressures involved in a family where she was preparing meals for ten people three times each day. She took full advantage of her good burning abilities and possessed the additional asset of leading an extremely active physical life in caring for eight children. (It is true that the more you do, the more you can eat.) Through careful weekly experimentation in gradually adding items not on her eating project to lose weight, she was able to indulge in the following one week's maximum maintenance, basing the selections on her own individual preferences:

Additions to her basic eating project
1. 6 crackers with cheese for evening snack (3 times)
2. 1 cup serving of a macaroni casserole (twice)
3. Salad dressings each day

Substitutions in her basic eating project
1. Pork products (bacon, sausage, ham) in one half the quantities she had been consuming of permitted proteins
2. 1 cup cold cereal in place of white bread and protein requirements at Meal #1 (twice)

Evelyn P. was not only able to successfully re-educate and rehabilitate her own attitudes about eating and become permanently slim, but through her excellent nutritional example, her husband and her eight children have become happily accustomed to eating a nutritionally balanced correct diet, and the chances of weight problems or nutritional imbalances occurring in the P. Family are small indeed.

Category 2: Fair achiever, male:

Everett C., single, age thirty, is a lineman for the telephone company. He lost 52½ pounds in eighteen weeks and maintained his weight exactly during five weeks of supervised maintenance. While this might seem to be a good achievement, it is in actuality only fair in his case, because he deviated fairly frequently from his planned eating project. In spite of this, he was able to lose weight steadily since he was a good burner,* was young, and was engaged in daily strenuous physical activity in his occupation. He found it difficult to retrain his deeply ingrained poor eating habits. As a bachelor, he was affected by many external pressures. He associated weekend dating with the consumption of alcoholic beverages, and week nights "out with the boys" were equated in his mind with potato chips, pretzels, and beer. He was often confronted with temptations to eat improperly through his connection with the local fire department and its many social functions, as well as through his attendance at telephone company dinners and meetings. Although he failed to put maximum effort into his eating project to lose weight, he did accomplish full results because of what he learned about himself and by his acquired ability to analyse his difficulties and apply this knowledge to his eating. He may experience recurring difficulties if he neglects his ability to be self-analytical and to think before he eats. Based on his own personal preferences, his maximum one week's maintenance must be slightly less than that of the good achiever:

Additions to his basic eating project
1. 3 beers
2. 3 slices pizza on Saturday night
3. One paper napkin full of potato chips
4. One paper napkin full of pretzels

---

* *Remember that a "good burner" is a person who loses even when not strictly following his eating project, and who could have lost much more.*

Substitutions in his basic eating project
1. Rye bread in place of white bread (once)
2. Hard roll in place of white bread (once)

Category 2: Fair achiever, female:

Sara W., age forty-two, married, with two adolescent children, lost twenty pounds in fourteen weeks. This put her fortunately a few pounds below the original weight goal she had set herself, because she gained four pounds during the first four weeks of her supervised maintenance. During the fifth week, however, she was able to lose three of those four pounds. The initial four-pound gain during maintenance occurred because she failed to experiment carefully in adding foods to her eating project and was too overconfident. This overconfidence can be dangerous. Sara W. tried her new wings too rapidly, so to speak, but she was able to correct this tendency before the five weeks of supervised maintenance were completed, because her overconfidence quickly turned to fear. She is employed as a secretary, which is a sedentary job, but this lack of activity is offset by the fact that she is socially and politically very active. She is an attractive, party-girl type, looking much younger than her forty-two years, especially since her loss of weight. Her loss of twenty pounds in fourteen weeks was only a fair achievement. Her difficulty lay in the fact that she felt she wasn't "that fat," and she often succumbed to the pressures surrounding her and found that it was not easy to lose steadily with all the deviating she was doing. When she changed her attitude and finally settled down to some thinking, she selected the following items for one week's maintenance:

Additions to her basic eating project
1. 3 Martinis
2. 2 small servings party hors d'oeuvres
3. 1 two-inch wedge of chocolate cake

Substitutions in her basic eating project
1. 4 medium pancakes at Sunday Meal #1 in place of
   bread and protein

Because of her business, political, and social endeavors, Sara W.'s new slim attractiveness is very important to her. She respects how she looks and how she feels, and is now able to handle her maintenance without any difficulties.

Category 3: Poor achiever, male:

Harry L., married, age forty-five, and a business executive, lost forty-two pounds in twenty-six weeks. During five weeks of supervised maintenance, he maintained this weight. For a male, this is classified as a poor achievement. Harry L.'s weeks of weight loss were often cancelled out by gains incurred because of eating problems brought about occupationally and by his inability to take his eating project to lose weight seriously enough. His losses were completely sporadic, and he often did not deserve to lose even what he did. He attended many business and civic banquets, traveled out of town on business trips, and went to many conventions. Because of this, he claimed he found proper eating most difficult. His active suburban social life also provided him with easy reasons for drifting away from his planned eating project. Saturday nights signified the choosing of a before and after restaurant when he went to the theatre, and entertaining friends and clients always involved excessive eating and drinking. He often succumbed to these social pressures, as testified by his intermittent gains and losses and his weeks of staying even. These business and social excuses are in reality fat copouts and are not necessarily valid, but in Harry L.'s case, he was unable to overcome the tendency to cheat badly in many of these situations. Reaching his desired weight goal consequently took much longer than was necessary, but he did finally accomplish this goal. His basic eating pattern had improved, although it was not entirely corrected as in the case of good and sometimes fair achievers. Since Harry L.'s life style will continue in its usual manner, he has less latitude in his maintenance, and he has, in fact, really been on maintenance all along! The following additions and substitutions, selected by him according to his personal preferences are permissible to him during a two-week period rather than in the usual one week:

Additions to his basic eating project
1. 3 whiskeys and soda
2. 2 small chocolate bars
3. Cocktail sauces with seafood (three times)

Substitutions in his basic eating project
1. Complete dinner in French restaurant (once)
2. Bagel with lox and cream cheese Sunday at Meal #1 in place of bread and protein allotment

Category 3: Poor achiever, female:

Grace M., a retired lady of sixty, lost thirty pounds in twenty-two weeks, and during five weeks of supervised maintenance, she lost an additional one and three quarters pounds. Grace M. was completely sedentary, and her emotional attitude was rigidly failure-oriented. Her motivation was poor, because she seemed disinterested in her appearance and was trying to lose weight only because her physician had insisted she do so for health reasons. With her aging body chemistry and her lifetime of poor eating habits, weight loss was a long, slow process, but eventually she began slowly to understand herself and her attitudes better. She realized how her Italian-American background had encouraged her appetite for oils, sauces, and pasta. As a poor achiever who engaged in considerable deviation during her weight-losing project, she is confined to a minimum maintenance. As she was cheating so much all the way through, she has little leeway left for extras. Common sense tells you that you cannot add to and add to, ad infinitum, without suffering the repercussions of a weight gain. Grace W. had really been on a semi-unsupervised maintenance all along. Of course, it was not total maintenance, or she would not have finally succeeded in losing thirty pounds. Based on the individual preferences of Grace M., a poor achiever, the following maintenance is for a two week period:

Additions to her basic eating project
1. 1 cup serving spaghetti (twice)
2. 3 small glasses of wine

Substitutions in her basic eating project
1. 1 slice pound cake in place of white bread (twice)

In all of the above cases, good achievers (male and female) fair achievers (male and female), and poor achievers (male and female), each of the individuals concerned is at present maintaining slimness without difficulty. Their basic eating patterns have either been completely corrected or have at least improved considerably. All exhibit a lack of interest in butter or margarine, fats, gravies, ketchup, and similar items that their appetites have been schooled away from. Each person became finally aware of exactly how he was eating to lose his unwanted extra weight, and, through supervised individual maintenance, learned exactly how much, how often, what, and when they could add or substitute. Their initial confusion has vanished, and they are no longer fooling themselves about their eating. They have placed eating in its proper perspective and have become independent eaters and thinkers.

The final two categories, non-achiever, male, and non-achiever, female, do not, in one sense, really belong with the others, because they consist of would-be weight losers who never made it to the maintenance stage. We hope all readers will exert every effort to avoid falling into either of these categories! These are the overweight persons who just were not sufficiently motivated to begin with, or were completely and inexorably failure oriented. They made little or no attempt to develop the three magic ingredients—courage, intelligence, and patience. On the contrary, they remained cowardly, stupid, and terribly impatient where weight loss was concerned. These attitudes breed failure. Never think negatively. Think positively, if you really want to be slim!

Category 4: Non-achiever, male:

Greg B. procrastinated with his eating project; took refuge in endless fat copouts; rationalized his failures constantly; and misplaced the blame for these failures.

He claimed he had gland trouble. (His doctor said he did not!) He insisted his wife had contributed to his failure. (She had nothing to do with it!) He pretended that his large and complex business demanded all of his time and energy, leaving no room for him to think or plan in his eating or his weight-losing project. (Ironically, Greg B. has recently suffered a severe heart attack because of his extreme obesity and is confined to a hospital. His business is disintegrating!) Greg B. is still fat.

Category 4: Non-achiever, female:

Dorothy Z. is a victim of utterly negative thinking. She has four young children and makes them the excuse for her inability to follow a correct eating project to lose weight. Because of the demands of the children, she has no time to bother about herself or her eating. (Sadly enough, all four of the children are fat, too— and that's a sin! Overweight mothers usually pass their poor eating habits on to their children.) She accuses her husband of being supercritical, which makes her too nervous to plan menus or shop properly. (She would be a lot more nervous if she knew her husband is running around with his slim secretary because his wife is so fat and unattractive!) She also feels that her large house requires the little time she has left over from her family to keep it in order. (In truth, her house is a mess. She would have much more energy if she rid herself of the fifty extra pounds she is lugging around!) Dorothy Z. is still fat and probably always will be.

As a matter of fact, you can easily pick out the non-achievers all by yourself. You will find them in every ice cream parlor and in every pizza stand, gorging themselves on enemy foods. They eat junk when they're depressed and when they're exhilarated; they eat junk when it rains and when the weather is fine; they eat junk to celebrate achievements and to mollify their problems. They are easy to identify. They all wear fat costumes: the women in size forty-two tent dresses, and the men in baggy suits with vast, flapping trousers. *Don't be one of them!*

As one further example of individual maintenance, we offer the personal maintenance programs of each of the authors. Both were good achievers and have maintained their slimness with ease and comfort for the past five years.

Murray J. Siegel lost not quite two hundred pounds in approximately eight months. His original hideous eating habits and difficulties have been so completely corrected that he has entirely lost his desires for enemy foods, and, in fact, for any foods that were not included in his eating project to lose weight. This change of attitude was not precipitated in any way by fear of regaining his lost weight, nor has he "psyched" himself into a dislike of junk foods. At the start of his maintenance project, he methodically tried all the enemy foods that had formerly so strongly appealed to him, only to find that he had totally lost his taste for them. He had acquired instead a definite taste for his unlimited "friends"— chiffon gelatin desserts, fresh fruits, vegetables, and so on. His personal maintenance, therefore, consists of additional quantities of allowables, whenever the occasion arises and he feels like having them:

Additions to his basic eating project
1. Extra cheese

2. Extra protein (meat, poultry, fish)
3. More than five fruits per day
4. Extra servings of limited vegetables (List C in Food Categories in Appendix A)

Murray J. Siegel has so re-educated and rehabilitated his eating and his attitudes that he now never drinks alcoholic beverages and eats no cake, candy, ice cream, gravies, potatoes, etc. He enjoys his meals, and he maintains his weight exactly.

Dolores van Keuren lost twenty-eight pounds in six weeks, which is an excellent achievement for a female. As further evidence of how completely individual a maintenance situation can be, it is most interesting that her personal maintenance project differs greatly from that of Murray J. Siegel. Although her basic eating pattern is now completely correct, she prefers to add and substitute as follows:

Additions to her basic eating project (weekly)
1. 2 martinis
2. 1 bowl popcorn with melted butter
3. 6 to 12 cookies
4. Candy (on a rare occasion)

Substitutions in her basic eating project
1. Pork products in one-half quantities of permitted proteins
2. Muffins or rolls in place of white bread

She, too, enjoys her meals, indulges in the above extras, and maintains her weight exactly.

FINAL MAINTENANCE INSTRUCTIONS:

1. Go over your Check List reviews.
2. Know your nutritional profile by analyzing your Weight Record Chart.
3. Determine whether you are a good achiever, a fair achiever, or a poor achiever, and review the maintenance of the appropriate cases, keeping in mind that your additions and substitutions will be based strictly on your own individual preferences.
4. Gradually add and substitute items not on your eating project to lose weight, weighing yourself once a week and duplicating weigh-in conditions as instructed.
5. If you show a gain at the end of the first week of this experimental maintenance, revert to your basic eating project to lose weight and follow it strictly for the next week; during the third week, add and substitute again, in slightly lesser quantities than the first week.
6. If you show a loss at the end of the first experimental maintenance week, add and substitute a bit more, being cautious and careful not to go to extremes.
7. If you stay even at the end of the first experimental maintenance week, allow yourself a similar quantity of extras for the next week, changing items to their equivalents if you wish.
8. If, at the completion of five weeks of self-supervised maintenance, you do not yet have an accurate idea of exactly how much, how often, and what you can add and substitute, spend a few more weeks following the same procedure. Five weeks is the norm for most people, but it is important to continue ex-

perimentally until you are sure of yourself and your ability to maintain your weight.

9. At the completion of your period of experimentation, continue to make a weight check once each week. If you exceed your maintenance and should gain a pound or two, resume your basic eating project to lose weight until you have shed those pounds. Try not to allow yourself to gain more than a pound or two at any given time. You may then resume your maintenance.

10. For your convenience in determining food values, we suggest that you consult the excellent books and pamphlets published by the United States Department of Agriculture, because we have found their statistics to be the most reliable and accurate. The fact that calories *do* count cannot be disregarded or disguised, but we believe that you cannot really count them. In fact, no two calorie-counting guides give the exact same calorie values for the same food items. Difficulties also arise because even exactly similar-appearing cuts of meat will have differing fat contents and thus differing calorie content; no two women cook in exactly the same manner; and the same food product manufactured by three different companies will have three different calorie values.

To be more specific, one scoop of vanilla ice cream and one hot fudge sundae with nuts and whipped cream obviously have vastly differing calorie contents, although both are ice cream desserts. Therefore, in adding and substituting in your individual maintenance project, be well aware that calories do count and be honest and realistic in your selections!

12. METAMORPHOSIS—THE MIRACLE OF THINKING THIN

Planning a balanced, nutritional eating project and then observing it takes a little working at, but it is well worth it. Plotting an experimental maintenance project for yourself takes a little working at, too, but it is also well worth it. The Think Thin process of losing weight permanently is not really all that difficult, it's just different. And that's where courage comes in. Overweight people are notoriously lacking in courage. Most of them are pathetic cowards when it comes to losing weight. The minute it gets different or the slightest bit difficult, they quit! That's cowardice! They use every conceivable copout to rationalize their failures. But everyone has *some* courage, and it can be called on. Many lucky people are slim by sheer accident. By making a courageous and determined effort with your weight problem, through a *realistic* project of good balanced eating and good balanced thinking, *you* can get slim and *stay* slim —by design! An improved mental attitude and a corrected eating pattern soon become automatic good habit and the initial concentrated effort is no longer required.

At the Think Thin schools, legions of formerly overweight people have attained permanent slimness. Now, by means of this book, which is really a manual for people interested in knowing more about individual nutrition to lose and/or to maintain weight, and the one preceeding it, *How To Be Suddenly Slim,* you can obtain the entire Think Thin philosophy. Fat people are, unfortunately, often downright confused where their eating and their thinking about eating are concerned. Most of them really know that there are fewer calories in an apple than in a chocolate brownie, yet they will persist in eating the brownie instead of the apple, and that's stupidity! The instructions are here, the knowhow is here, the recipes are here, the experience and encouragement are here—all spelled out in detail. Use your *intelligence* to apply this unique and invaluable information to your own weight problem. The purpose of this book is to destroy fat copouts and to remove the major stumbling blocks.

And you really can get suddenly slim; suddenly in comparison with the length of time you have probably endured the burden of overweight. Have the *patience* to see it through to the end. There is no instant, overnight miracle available to the overweight, despite the optimistic and often fraudulent advertising that appears in almost every American publication these days. But as the weeks of your eating project go by, the lost pounds add up, the alterations in thinking add up, and there you are—suddenly and permanently slim! For an overweight person, that *is* a miracle—the greatest miracle of all. You will have performed your own individual magic.

Develop the three magic ingredients—courage, intelligence, and patience—and work this miracle for yourself. You'll feel wonderful. You'll look great. You'll walk with dignity and self-respect. You'll be, in a sense, reborn. Courage, intelligence, and patience can give you a new life. Murray J. Siegel, once a grotesque fat man, lives now as a slim, dynamic individual. Dolores van Keuren, once well on her way toward a fat and matronly middle age, has turned back the clock with a loss of almost thirty pounds. You, too, can be suddenly slim. You can live for the first time. Really live. Trade in your own private fat Hell for a new lease on life!

THINK
thin
MENUS

THINK THIN MENUS

HOW MURRAY J. SIEGEL ATE TO LOSE NOT QUITE 200 POUNDS

MEAL NUMBER 1:

CHOOSE ONLY ONE:

> Small portion meat, poultry, or fish
> 1 egg
> 1 slice cheese (American, Swiss, Cheddar, etc.)
> Small portion cottage cheese

Beverage (Optional)

A MUST: 2 slices regular enriched white bread

MEAL NUMBER 2:

CHOOSE ONLY ONE:

> Medium portion meat, poultry, or fish
> Small portion tuna or salmon (*not* water-packed)
> 2 eggs
> 2 slices cheese (American, Swiss, Muenster, etc.)
> Medium portion cottage cheese

Vegetables under Lists B and C (See Food Categories)

Beverage (Optional)

A MUST: 2 slices regular enriched white bread

MEAL NUMBER 3:

Large portion meat, poultry, or fish
Vegetables under Lists B and C (See Food Categories)
Beverage (Optional)

ADDITIONAL INSTRUCTIONS:

A MUST: 1 pint skim milk daily
OPTIONAL: 5 fruits daily
Tomato juice is *not* a fruit. ($\frac{1}{2}$ cup tomato juice $=\frac{1}{2}$ cup
   vegetable)
Skin of poultry *not* to be eaten.
No corn.
No more than 5 eggs a week
No tongue or brisket pot roast
FISH IS ENTIRELY OPTIONAL

**HOW DOLORES VAN KEUREN
ATE TO LOSE 28 POUNDS**

MEAL NUMBER 1:

CHOOSE ONLY ONE:
   Small portion meat, poultry, or fish
   1 egg
   1 slice cheese (American, Swiss, Cheddar, etc.)
   Small portion cottage cheese
Beverage (Optional)
A MUST: 1 slice regular enriched white bread

MEAL NUMBER 2:

CHOOSE ONLY ONE:
    Medium portion meat, poultry, or fish
    Small portion tuna or salmon (*not* water packed)
    2 eggs
    2 slices cheese (American, Swiss, Muenster, etc.)
    Medium portion cottage cheese
Vegetables under Lists B and C (See Food Categories)
Beverage (Optional)
A MUST: 1 slice regular enriched white bread

MEAL NUMBER 3:

Large portion meat, poultry, or fish
Vegetables under Lists B and C (See Food Categories)
Beverage (Optional)

ADDITIONAL INSTRUCTIONS:

A MUST: 1 pint skim milk daily
OPTIONAL: 3 fruits daily
Tomato juice is *not* a fruit. (½ cup tomato juice = ½ cup
    vegetable)
Skin of poultry *not* to be eaten.
No corn.
No more than 5 eggs a week
No tongue or brisket pot roast
FISH IS ENTIRELY OPTIONAL

FOOD CATEGORIES

Murray J. Siegel says: "I confined myself to these categories in making up my menus."

1. Proteins:

Lean beef	Rock Cornish Hen
Lean lamb	Shellfish
Veal	Fish
Chicken	All beef franks
Turkey	

Cottage, Farmer, Pot, or Ricotta cheese
American, Swiss, Cheddar, Muenster cheese, etc.
Eggs

(*Note:* The exceptions are tongue, pot roast, and pork of any kind. My research revealed that tongue is extremely high in caloric content; pot roast cooks in its own fat juices; and pork is excessively greasy and fatty. I consumed very little fish other than lobster, shrimp, or tuna, and those only on rare occasions. Although some sources stress a preponderance of fish, I found this to be unimportant in my case. If you enjoy fish, eat it, of course, as part of your menu variation. For me, varying *all* my foods was the most significant factor.)

2. Carbohydrates:
    Enriched white bread

(*Note:* I used absolutely no butter, margarine, oil, fat, gravies or sugar of any kind.)

3. Milk:
    I consumed one pint of skim milk each day.

4. Unlimited allowables:

List A:

Low-calorie carbonated beverages

Coffee	Pepper
Tea	Vinegar
Water	All spices
Bouillon	All herbs
Seltzer	Lemon
Horseradish	Lime
Salt	Mustard

(*Note:* All items in List A may be consumed at meals or between meals in unlimited quantities unless you are personally restricted.)

5. Vegetables:

List B:	Water cress
Celery	Asparagus
Cucumber	Cabbage
Dill pickles	Cauliflower
Spinach	Pimientos
French style string bean	Summer squash (yellow)
Parsley	Zucchini squash
Radishes	Endive
Lettuce	Chinese cabbage
Green peppers	Sauerkraut
Broccoli	Bean sprouts
Escarole	Beet greens
Mushrooms	Mustard greens
Swiss chard	Kale
Chicory	Turnip tops

(*Note:* I refer to these as "minus-calorie" items because I found that for me, these vegetables had little of significance that was detrimental to my weight loss. I considered them to be *unlimited* and ate as much as I wanted at meals or between meals.)

List C:	Mature green beans
Onion	Okra
Carrots	Pumpkin
Beets	Turnips
Tomato	Parsnips
Peas	Scallions
Artichokes	Oyster plant
Brussels sprouts	Bamboo shoots
Eggplant	Jerusalem artichokes
Squash	Tomato juice

(*Note:* I allowed myself one small serving (approximately ½ cup) each day at *any* meal.)

6. Fruits:

I found that fresh fruits, in season, made satisfying desserts at meals and were a good choice for between-meal snacking. I stayed away from bananas, grapes, cherries, watermelon, and dried fruits.)

(*Note:* I used *no* mayonnaise or ketchup, but I did permit myself small amounts of Worcestershire sauce, A-1 sauce, and soy sauce for seasoning purposes where necessary.)

21 CONSECUTIVE DAYS SAMPLE MENUS

MEAL NUMBER ONE   21 CONSECUTIVE DAYS

The suggested eating pattern outlined below is the basis for the twenty-one menus which follow it. Use it as a guide to plan your own Meal number 1 menus.

SUGGESTED EATING PATTERN FOR MEAL NUMBER 1:

Fruit

Regular enriched white bread (men, 2 slices; women, 1 slice)

Any vegetables as desired from List B (see Food Categories)

Choose only *one* of the following, varying each day:

1. 1 egg
2. Small portion meat, fish, or poultry
3. About ⅓ cup cottage cheese
4. 1 slice cheese (American, Swiss, Muenster, Cheddar, etc.)

Beverage

(*Note:* These menus are similar to those followed by Murray J. Siegel to lose almost two hundred pounds in approximately eight months, and by Dolores van Keuren to lose twenty-eight pounds in six weeks. Murray consumed two slices of regular enriched white bread at Meal #1, and Dolores consumed one slice).

(Asterisks refer to recipes detailed in the Recipe Section. See Index for page numbers.)

Day number 1:

½ grapefruit
Small broiled hamburger patty with onion slice
Toast
Beverage

Day number 2:

Baked apple*
Open-faced Danish Delight*
Beverage

Day number 3:

Sectioned navel orange
1 broiled lamb chop
Toast
Beverage

Day number 4:

Rosy baked pear*
Oysters Millicent on toast*
Beverage

Day number 5:

Low-calorie orange soda
1 broiled all beef hotdog
Toast
Beverage

Day number 6

Small glass tomato juice
Open-faced Chicken Supreme*
Beverage

Day number 7:

½ canteloupe
Small broiled lamb patty with broiled tomato slice
Toast
Beverage

Day number 8:

½ grapefruit
1 Veal roll*
Toast
Beverage

Day number 9:

Small glass orange juice
Sliced turkey
Toast
Beverage

Day number 10:

Baked apple*
Leftover sliced steak, heated, on toast
Beverage

Day number 11:

Pineapple Ambrosia*
⅓ can tuna, flaked, on toast
Beverage

Day number 12:

Sliced navel orange
Small broiled chicken breast (leftover)
Toast
Beverage

Day number 13:

½ grapefruit
Eastern Omelet*
Toast
Beverage

Day number 14:

Small glass tomato juice
"Danish Pastry"*
Beverage

Day number 15:

Rosy Baked Pear*
Coney Island Hot Dog*
Toast
Beverage

Day number 16:

Pineapple Ambrosia*
Sliced cold roast chicken
Toast
Beverage

Day number 17:

Tangerine
Scrambled hamburg*

Toast
Beverage

Day number 18:

½ canteloupe
Pizza*
Beverage

Day number 19:

Small glass tomato juice
1 broiled veal chop
Toast
Beverage

Day number 20:

Sliced orange
Mushroom Omelet*
Toast
Beverage

Day number 21:

½ grapefruit
1 slice leftover meat loaf*
Toast
Beverage

SAMPLE MENUS

MEAL NUMBER TWO   21 CONSECUTIVE DAYS

The suggested eating pattern outlined below is the basis for the twenty-one menus which follow it. Use it as a guide to plan your own Meal number 2 menus.

SUGGESTED EATING PATTERN FOR MEAL NUMBER 2:

Regular enriched white bread (men, 2 slices; women, 1 slice)

Any vegetables as desired from List B (see Food Categories)

Choose only *one* of the following, varying each day:

1. 2 eggs
2. Medium portion meat, fish, or poultry
3. About ⅔ cup cottage cheese
4. 2 slices cheese (American, Swiss, Muenster, Cheddar, etc.)

Beverage

Optional: Fruit or a Think Thin dessert (See Recipe Section)

Keep in mind the injunctions against too much cheese or too many eggs. When you do elect cheese remember that cottage cheese and the hard cheeses are permissible, while the soft, spreadable cheeses are not.

Allowed	*Avoid*
Cottage cheese	Cheese Whiz
Farmer cheese	Velveeta
Pot cheese	Camembert
Ricotta	All cheese spreads
American	
Swiss	
Cheddar	
Muenster	
Mozzarella	
Hard Italian cheeses	

SAMPLE MENUS

MEAL NUMBER TWO   21 CONSECUTIVE DAYS

Asterisks used in the menus refer to recipes detailed in the Recipe Section. See Index for page numbers.

Day number 1:

Mushroom Soup*
Salmon Casserole*
Tossed green salad
Salad Dressing Piquant*
Beverage

Day number 2:

Scrambled Hamburg*
Stuffed Pepper Salad*
Toast
Beverage

Day number 3:

Cream of Spinach Soup*
Cheese Soufflé
Orange Chiffon* with Lo-Whip*
Beverage

Day number 4:

Mug of hot beef bouillon
Asparagus Omelet*
Toast
Large apple

Day number 5:

Bean Sprout Soup*
Mustard Tuna*
Celery sticks
Toast
Beverage

Day number 6:

Madrilène Soup*
½ canteloupe filled with ½ cup cottage cheese, sprinkled
    with a few blueberries
Toast
Beverage

Day number 7:

Chicken Pizzacante*
Canned French-style string beans
Toast
Beverage

Day number 8:

Mushroom Omelet*
Tossed green salad
Salad Dressing Italiano*
Toast
Beverage

Day number 9:

Spring Garden Salad*
Vegetable Soup*
White bread
Beverage

Day number 10:

Cream of Asparagus Soup*
Open-faced Chicken Supreme*
Black Cherry Chiffon*
Beverage

Day number 11:

German Frankfurters with Sauerkraut*
White bread
Pineapple Ambrosia*
Beverage

Day number 12:

Bean Sprout Soup*
Open-faced Danish Delight*
Celery sticks
Beverage

Day number 13:

1 Stuffed Pepper*
Zippy Cole Slaw*
Toast
Beverage

Day number 14:

Chopped Chicken Liver* in bed of lettuce
Sliced tomato and onion
Dill pickles
Toast
Beverage

Day number 15:

Peppers à la Monaco*
Salad Delight*
Toast
Beverage

Day number 16:

Mushroom Soup*
Broiled hamburger with onion slice
Hearts of lettuce with lemon
Toast
Beverage

Day number 17:

Deviled Eggs*
Pickled Bean Salad*
Dill pickles
Toast
Beverage

Day number 18:

Turkey sandwich with lettuce
Celery sticks & green pepper rings
Carvel*
Beverage

Day number 19:

Mug of chicken bouillon
Shrimp Salad*
Toast
Custard Treat*
Beverage

Day number 20:

Medium broiled Chicken Breast Italiano*
Spinach Louise*
White bread
Raspberry Chiffon*
Beverage

Day number 21:

Cheese Soufflé*
Spicy Pickled Beets*
Cucumber wedges
Baked Pear*
Beverage

SAMPLE MENUS

MEAL NUMBER THREE 21 CONSECUTIVE DAYS

The suggested eating pattern outlined below is the basis for the twenty-one menus which follow it. Use it as a guide to plan your own Meal number 3 menus.

SUGGESTED EATING PATTERN FOR MEAL NUMBER 3:

Optional: Soup (See Recipe Section)
Large portion meat, fish, or poultry
At least two unlimited vegetables from List B (See food categories in Menu Section).
One ½-cup serving of a limited vegetable from List C (See Menu Section)
Large salad
Beverage
Optional: Fruit or a Think Thin Dessert (See Recipe Section)

As stated before, the limited vegetable from List C is really optional at this meal. It has been suggested at this meal because Meal number 3, being the largest of the day, seems to leave more room for this limited vegetable. However, the ½ cup of a vegetable from List C may be consumed at Meal number 1 or Meal number 2 or eliminated entirely. This is up to individual discretion.

Permissible desserts will be found under the heading Desserts in the Recipe Section. All fruit is entirely optional. If desired, men may have five pieces of fruit each day, either at meals or between meals. Women may have three pieces. The rule of variation also applies to fruit. Make sure that each serving of fruit is different within a given day. The following fruits should be avoided:

Bananas	Watermelon
Grapes	Avocado
Cherries	Dried fruits

MEAL NUMBER THREE 21 CONSECUTIVE DAYS

(Asterisks refer to recipes detailed in the Recipe Section. See Index for page numbers.)

Day number 1:

Antipasto Think Thin*
Chicken Cacciatore*
Leaf spinach
Yellow summer squash
Hearts of lettuce with lemon wedges
Black Cherry Chiffon Gelatin*
Beverage

Day number 2:

Parsley-vegetable bouillon*
Veal Balls*
Baked Acorn Squash*
French-style string beans

Sweet and sour Cucumber Salad*
Sliced navel orange
Beverage

Day number 3:

Chicken with Mushrooms*
Broccoli stalks
Whole baby carrots
Asparagus spears
Tossed green salad with two tablespoons "Sour Cream"
    Salad Dressing*
Custard Treat*
Beverage

Day number 4:

Leftover-Broccoli Soup*
Roast beef
Green peas
French-style waxed beans
Zippy Cole Slaw*
½ Broiled grapefruit
Beverage

Day number 5:

Whole Rock Cornish hen
"Mashed Potatoes"*
Beets
Asparagus cuts
Perfection Salad*
Strawberry Sherbet*
Beverage

Day number 6:

Cream of Asparagus Soup*
Broiled lamb patties
Mushrooms Sauté*
Minted Carrots*
French-style string beans
Pineapple Ambrosia*
Beverage

Day number 7:

Lobster Chun King*
Kale
Hearts of Artichoke Salad*
Tangy Orange Mold*
Beverage

Day number 8:

Roast turkey
Cranberry Relish*
Spinach Louise*
Sweet and Sour Red Cabbage*
Tossed green salad with Garlic Vinegar*
Apple Pie*
Beverage

Day number 9:

Broiled steak
"Mashed Potatoes"*
Green peas
Relish platter
Pineapple Sherbet*
Beverage

136

Day number 10:

Small Chopped Chicken Liver* appetizer with radish roses
Shrimp Creole*
Bean sprouts
Cabbage Suisse*
Custard Treat*
Beverage

Day number 11:

Tropical Chicken*
Zucchini Firenze*
Garlic Artichoke*
Sweet and Sour Cucumber Salad*
Raspberry Chiffon* with Lo-Whip*
Beverage

Day number 12:

Chinese Pepper Steak* on bed of bean sprouts
Snow peas
Hearts of lettuce with wine vinegar
Strawberries Jubilee*
Beverage

Day number 13:

Cream of Spinach Soup*
Bayou Casserole*
Perfection Salad*
Baked Apple*
Beverage

Day number 14:

Veal Rolls*
Baked Acorn Squash*

Braised Celery*
Pickled Bean Salad*
½ broiled grapefruit
Beverage

Day number 15:

Mushroom Soup*
Roast chicken
Turnip Whip*
Asparagus spears
Fresh fruit salad on lettuce leaf
Beverage

Day number 16:

Pompano Marinara*
Yellow summer squash
Spinach Louise*
Hearts of Artichoke Salad*
Fresh grapefruit and orange sections
Beverage

Day number 17:

Vegetable Bouillon*
Roast turkey roll
Cranberry Relish*
French-style string beans
Broccoli Espagnole*
Escarole salad
Orange Sherbet*
Beverage

Day number 18:

Horseradish Beef Bake*
Gourmet Cabbage*
Cauliflower Special*
Stop and Go Salad*
Baked Pear*
Beverage

Day number 19:

Antipasto Think Thin*
Chicken Pizzacante*
Baked Zucchini*
French-style waxed beans
Pineapple Ambrosia*
Beverage

Day number 20:

Cream of Spinach Soup*
Mushroom Meat Loaf*
Broccoli spears
Tomato, onion, and lettuce salad
Orange Chiffon* with Lo-Whip*
Beverage

Day number 21:

Lobster tails broiled with lemon
Braised Celery*
Spinach Louise*
Sweet and Sour Cucumber Salad*
½ canteloupe filled with Pineapple Sherbet*
Beverage

THINK
thin
RECIPES

THINK THIN®RECIPES

You can lose weight and keep it off by placing eating in its proper perspective, and as a result, your attitude about eating and your eating habits will change. You will find that you are actually eating more food* than you ever did before, that you are enjoying your meals, and that, best of all, you are steadily losing weight. It takes thinking and a little work, but the magnificent results will speak for themselves. And those results are dignity, self-respect, and a feeling of accomplishment, adding up to a new slim you!

Although the recipes that follow are neither complicated nor time-consuming, you will find them tasty, attractive, satisfying, and rewarding. This way of eating is not difficult, it is merely different and exciting.

Food is meat, fish, poultry, eggs, cheese, bread, milk, fresh fruits, and fresh vegetables. . . . not enemy or junk foods!

EGGS

Note: We suggest that no more than 5 eggs be consumed each week, and that eggs be served only at Meal number 1 and Meal number 2.
Meal number 1: 1 egg
Meal number 2: 2 eggs

(Recipes specifying 1 egg are doubled for Meal number 2.)

POACHED EGG

  1 egg
  ¼ teaspoon salt
  ½ teaspoon vinegar
  Boiling water

Add salt and vinegar to water in shallow pan. Break egg into a cup. When water boils, stir vigorously, making water swirl in a spiral. Slide egg into swirling water. (This keeps the egg's shape.) Turn heat down. Poach 2 to 3 minutes for a soft egg, 3 to 5 minutes for a firmer egg. Serve on dry white toast.

EGG FLORENTINE

Prepare frozen chopped spinach according to directions on package, poach egg as above and serve in a nest of cooked chopped spinach. Sprinkle with freshly ground black pepper.

SCRAMBLED EGG

1 egg	½ teaspoon Worcestershire sauce
¼ teaspoon salt	1 tablespoon water or skim milk
⅛ teaspoon pepper	

Place all ingredients in bowl. Beat with a fork. Pour into preheated Teflon skillet without adding fat of any kind. Stir eggs until they are the consistency you prefer.

FRIED EGG

Break egg into preheated Teflon skillet without adding fat. Cook until edges begin to brown. Serve sunnyside up or turn and cook other side briefly.

BOILED EGG

Lower egg slowly into boiling water. An ice-cold egg may crack, so we suggest removing egg from refrigerator earlier to allow it to come to room temperature. Turn heat down. Cook 3 to 4 minutes for very soft egg, 5 minutes for medium egg, and 15 minutes for hard egg.

DEVILED EGGS   (Meal number 2)

2 hard-boiled eggs
1 to 2 teaspoons skim milk
1 to 2 teaspoons tomato juice
Few drops Worcestershire sauce
¼ teaspoon paprika

Halve eggs lengthwise. Remove yolks and mash with skim milk, tomato juice, and Worcestershire sauce. Fill egg whites with mixture and sprinkle with paprika.

PANCAKE

1 egg   1 capful vanilla extract
1 slice white bread   1 tablespoon water or skim milk

Place all ingredients in blender. Blend until liquid. Fry in heavy skillet without adding fat until pancake is browned on both sides.

VEGETABLE PANCAKE

1 egg   ½ cup Vegetable Pie* (See Index.)
1 slice white toast

Place all ingredients in blender. Blend until liquid. Fry in heavy skillet without adding fat until browned on both sides.

FRENCH TOAST

1 egg   1 teaspoon water or skim milk
¼ teaspoon nutmeg   1 slice white bread
¼ teaspoon cinnamon

Beat first 4 ingredients with fork. Soak bread in mixture until all liquid is absorbed. Broil on both sides on aluminum foil. (For toppings to serve with French Toast, see heading: Dessert Sauces, in Recipe Section.)

INSTANT BREAKFAST

1 cup skim milk
1 egg
½ teaspoon vanilla extract
⅛ teaspoon nutmeg
Artificial sweetener to taste

Blend all ingredients for a few seconds.

PEPPERS À LA MONACO

2 frying peppers, sliced thin
1 4½-ounce can Italian-style tomatoes
2 eggs
Salt and pepper

Put peppers and tomatoes in heavy skillet. Cook together until peppers are tender. Add 2 well-beaten eggs and salt and pepper to taste. Cook until eggs are set. (Equals Meal number 2 and includes 1 limited vegetable from List C.)

CHINESE CHICKEN EGG DROP

2 cups water
2 cubes or envelopes chicken bouillon
1 well-beaten egg

Dissolve chicken bouillon cubes or powder in water. Bring to boil and very slowly drop in beaten egg. Simmer 3 to 5 minutes.

EASTERN OMELET

1 egg
2 tablespoons chopped green pepper
1 teaspoon minced onion
¼ teaspoon Worcestershire sauce
Salt and pepper to taste
1 tablespoon water or skim milk

Place all ingredients in blender at low speed to mix. Fry in preheated Teflon skillet, lifting edges to allow liquid to run under until done. Fold and serve.

CHICKEN OMELET

⅓ cup diced cooked chicken
1 tablespoon diced onion
2 tablespoons chopped green pepper
1 egg
Salt and pepper to taste
1 tablespoon skim milk

Sauté onion and green pepper in tiny amount water until tender. Add diced chicken. Cook 2 minutes. Add egg beaten with milk, salt, and pepper. Cover and cook until set. Turn and cook other side in similar manner. (Meal number 2.)

MUSHROOM OMELET

1 egg, separated
1 small can mushroom pieces, drained
1 tablespoon water
Salt and pepper to taste

Preheat oven to 400°. Preheat Teflon skillet. Separate egg. Beat white until thick. Beat yolk, water, salt, and pepper until mixture is thick and lemon yellow. Fold in white. Fry in preheated skillet until bottom is light brown. Sprinkle mushrooms over top surface and slide into 400° oven for 3 to 5 minutes until top browns very lightly.

ASPARAGUS OMELET

1 egg
1 small can asparagus cuts, drained
1 teaspoon grated onion
Salt and pepper to taste

Mix well and cook in preheated heavy skillet.

STRAWBERRY OMELET

2 eggs
½ cup skim milk
1 slice white bread
¼ teaspoon salt
6 whole strawberries, sliced thin

Soak bread in ¼ cup of the milk. Mash with fork until very fine mixture, like cornmeal. Beat in eggs, salt, and remaining milk. Preheat Teflon skillet and slide mixture into skillet along sides so egg remains almost dry on top surface. Put a few drops artificial sweetener on strawberries and spread them on top of egg. Turn and cook well on both sides. (Equals Meal number 2 and includes one of the daily fruits.)

TOAD-IN-A-HOLE

1 egg
1 slice white toast

With juice glass, press into center of slice of toast and cut out a circle. Lay slice of toast in preheated Teflon skillet and break 1 egg into hole. When set, turn and cook on other side. Serve with egg covered with toast circle.

LUNCHBOX SPECIAL

2 hard-boiled eggs
3 radishes
Bread coated very thinly with mustard
Salt and pepper to taste

Cover bread with thinly sliced hard boiled eggs and radishes. Sprinkle with salt and pepper.

BLUEBERRY PANCAKES

  1 egg
  1 slice bread
  ¼ cup skim milk
  Pinch of cinnamon
  Artificial sweetener to taste
  ½ cup blueberries

Blend all ingredients except blueberries in blender. Pour batter into mixing bowl and fold in blueberries. Heat Teflon frying pan and spoon in batter to make pancakes. Fry on one side until done. Flip and fry on other side.

FISH

Note: A preponderance of fish meals is definitely *not* an absolute requirement for losing weight. The authors personally ate very little fish and worked with many obese people who were allergic to fish of any kind. These people were able to lose weight successfully and permanently although they consumed no fish at all. If you enjoy fish, however, it can be an excellent means of varying your meals.

HALIBUT BAKE

  2 halibut steaks
  Salt and pepper
  1 8-ounce can tomato sauce
  1 teaspoon minced onion
  1 tablespoon parsley flakes
  ¼ teaspoon garlic salt
  Lemon wedges

Preheat oven to 350°. Season fish with salt and pepper; place in baking dish. Combine tomato sauce, onion, parsley, and garlic salt. Pour over fish. Bake about 40 minutes. Serve with lemon wedges. (Equals Meal number 3 for 2 and includes one limited vegetable from List C.)

FABULOUS FLOUNDER

1 pound flounder fillets
Salt, pepper, paprika,
   garlic powder

1 cup chicken bouillon
   made from cube or
   powder
2 tablespoons powdered
   skim milk

Preheat oven to 400°. Put fish in baking dish and sprinkle generously with seasonings. Add powdered skim milk to chicken bouillon and pour over fish. Bake for 15 minutes in hot oven.

STUFFED BAKED FISH FILLETS

4 fish fillets (about 1 pound)
1 tablespoon tomato purée
1 clove minced garlic
Salt and pepper
Mushroom Stuffing (See Index.)
Lemon slices

Preheat oven to 350°. Mix tomato purée and minced garlic. Wipe fish fillets and spread flat. Brush with tomato-garlic mixture and sprinkle with salt and pepper. Spread mushroom stuffing on each fillet. Roll and fasten with toothpicks. Bake in flat shallow pan for about 30 minutes. Garnish with lemon slices.

HADDOCK SURPRISE

Medium piece of haddock
1 slice Swiss cheese
Paprika

Broil haddock on one side. Turn. Lay Swiss cheese on top and sprinkle with paprika. Broil slowly until cheese is melted and bubbly. (Meal number 2)

SALMON OR TUNA CASSEROLE

1 3½-ounce can salmon or tuna,
    regular oil-packed
1 slice white bread
¼ cup chopped celery
¼ cup chopped green pepper
1 slice onion
1 tablespoon lemon juice

Preheat oven to 350°. Put bread in blender to make crumbs. Remove. Then place vegetables in blender. Remove and add to rest of ingredients in an individual casserole. Bake for 15 minutes.

MUSTARD TUNA

1 3½-ounce can tuna,
    regular oil-packed
2 tablespoons prepared
    mustard
1 slice onion, diced
1 stalk celery, diced
Salt and pepper
1 whole green pepper
3 radishes
½ cucumber, sliced

Mix first 5 ingredients thoroughly. Cut top off green pepper and remove seeds. Stuff with tuna mixture. Serve on bed of lettuce. Garnish with radish roses and cucumber slices.

BAYOU CASSEROLE

4 thick fish fillets
1 package frozen French-
style string beans,
thawed
½ cup sliced fresh mush-
rooms
½ cup diced green pepper
½ cup diced celery

¼ cup tomato juice
¼ teaspoon pepper
½ teaspoon salt
1 teaspoon onion
powder
1 envelope vegetable
bouillon, or 1 cube

Preheat oven to 350°. Spread string beans, mushrooms, green pepper, and celery in bottom of large deep casserole. Lay fish fillets on top of vegetable mixture. Mix tomato juice, salt, pepper, onion powder, and envelope of bouillon. Pour evenly over fish. Bake about 45 minutes.

OYSTERS MILLICENT

1 4-ounce can oysters
and juice
¼ cup water

½ cup skim milk
Salt and pepper
1 slice white toast

Chop oysters fine. Cook in juice and water approximately 5 minutes, or until liquid is almost absorbed. Add milk, salt, and pepper. Heat. Pour over toast in soup dish. (Vary amount of oysters according to Meal number 1 or Meal number 2. Men, 2 slices toast; women, 1 slice.)

POMPANO MARINARA

Pompano fish fillets (1 large fillet per person)
Marinara Sauce (See Index.)
1 large green pepper cut up
½ lb. fresh mushrooms, sliced

153

Simmer peppers and mushrooms slowly in Marinara Sauce. Pour mixture over fish fillets and broil for 15 to 20 minutes.

BAKED CLAMS

    1 8-ounce can minced clams
    1 slice bread
    ½ teaspoon grated Parmesan or Romano cheese
    ½ teaspoon garlic powder
    2 teaspoons minced onion
    ½ teaspoon Italian seasoning

Preheat oven to 350°. Drain clams. Use half the can for one serving. Toast bread and crumb in blender. (Save small amount of crumbs for topping.) Mix all ingredients and mound into large clam shells or in small baking dish. Sprinkle with reserved crumbs and a tiny pinch more cheese. Bake for 15 to 20 minutes.

LOBSTER CHUN KING

    1 cup lobster meat
    1 can bean sprouts
    2 stalks celery, chopped
    2 slices onion, chopped
    1 can mushroom slices
    1 envelope chicken bouillon power, or 1 cube

Mix all ingredients except lobster meat and cook slowly until tender. Add lobster meat and continue cooking 10 minutes.

BAKED FISH

1 pound any kind of fish
Salt, pepper, onion powder, paprika, garlic powder
Juice of 1 lemon

Mix the spices and season fish thoroughly. Squeeze lemon juice over fish. Refrigerate for 1 hour. Then bake at 350° for 30 minutes, basting occasionally with juice that forms in pan.

SCALLOPS PAPRIKA

1 pound bay scallops   Paprika, salt, pepper

Spread scallops in broiler pan. Sprinkle liberally with paprika, salt, and pepper. Broil close to flame 5 minutes. Then turn and broil additional five minutes. Serve with lemon wedges and parsley garnish.

CRAB CASSEROLE ALASKA

½ cup Alaska king crab   ½ cup skim milk
  meat   ⅛ teaspoon nutmeg
1 slice American cheese   1 slice toast

Preheat oven to 350°. Grate cheese and mix with crab meat, milk, and nutmeg. Bake until bubbly and slightly browned. Serve over slice of toast. (Meal number 2)

SEAFOOD AU GRATIN

½ pound lobster meat   ½ cup skim milk
½ pound cooked shrimp   Salt and pepper
2 slices American cheese   ½ teaspoon paprika

155

Preheat oven to 350°. Grate cheese and melt in skim milk in top of double boiler. Combine with lobster and shrimp, salt, and pepper. Place in baking casserole. Sprinkle with paprika. Bake for 20 minutes.

POACHED SOLE BOUQUETS

1 pound fillet of sole	6 whole peppercorns
Package frozen	3 bay leaves
broccoli spears	2 tablespoons dried
2 quarts water	onion flakes
½ cup white vinegar	Few sprigs parsley
1 teaspoon salt	

Wrap fish fillets around broccoli spears and secure with toothpicks. Set in shallow pan. Combine all other ingredients and bring to boil. Pour this liquid over fish and simmer slowly for 12 minutes.

TUNA MOLD

1 can tuna	Salt and pepper
1 envelope unflavored	1 cup diced celery
gelatin	1 teaspoon mustard
1¾ cups skim milk	1½ teaspoons lemon juice
2 egg yolks	½ cup diced pimientos

Mix gelatin with ½ cup of the milk. Mix remaining milk, egg yolks, salt and pepper and add to first mixture. Cook for 5 minutes, stirring constantly. Chill 1½ hours. Mix tuna with celery, mustard, lemon juice, and pimientos. Layer first and second mixtures in one-quart mold. Chill well. (Medium portion for Meal number 2.)

SHRIMP SALAD

3 ounces cooked, cleaned shrimp
2 tablespoons cottage cheese
1 stalk celery, diced
1 slice onion, diced
Salt and pepper

Toss all ingredients lightly. Serve on bed of crisp lettuce.
Garnish with green pepper rings.

SHRIMP MARINARA

1 pound boiled, cleaned shrimp
Small can tiny green peas
1 cup Marinara Sauce (See Index.)

Preheat oven to 350°. Mix all ingredients in casserole.
Bake for 20 minutes. (Includes 1 limited vegetable from
List C.)

SHRIMP SURPRISE

¾ cup cooked, cleaned shrimp
1 whole medium tomato
1 small can asparagus pieces
1 tablespoon diced celery
1 tablespoon chopped chives
1 tablespoon lemon juice
Salt and pepper

Core and partially quarter tomato. Place in bed of lettuce.
Mix all other ingredients and spoon into center of tomato.
Chill. (Includes 1 limited vegetable from List C.)

SHRIMP CREOLE

1 pound cooked, cleaned shrimp
1 medium onion, sliced
¼ cup chopped green pepper
Small can sliced mushrooms
Salt and pepper to taste
¼ teaspoon paprika
¼ teaspoon sage
⅛ teaspoon liquid sweetener, or equivalent
¼ cup canned tomato sauce
1 cup drained canned tomatoes
¼ teaspoon curry powder

Simmer together onion, green pepper, mushrooms, salt, pepper, paprika, sage and artificial sweetener in the tomato sauce until tender. Add canned tomatoes, shrimp, and curry powder. Heat.

BAKED STRIPED BASS

1 cleaned striped bass
1 large onion, sliced
1 medium can tomatoes
½ teaspoon rosemary
Salt and pepper

Preheat oven to 350°. Lay bass in baking dish. Lay onion slices over fish. Pour can of tomatoes over and sprinkle with rosemary and salt and pepper. Bake about 45 minutes or until fish is tender. Baking time will of course depend on size of fish.

TUNA OR SALMON PLATTER

1 individual can tuna or salmon
Lettuce
Radish roses
Green pepper rings
Cucumber slices
Garlic vinegar (See Index.)

Turn out fish onto bed of lettuce. Surround with radish roses, green pepper rings, and cucumber slices. Sprinkle with garlic vinegar.

TUNA OR SALMON SALAD

1 individual can tuna or salmon
½ cup chopped celery
2 tablespoons cottage cheese
1 tablespoon minced onion
Salt and pepper

Toss all ingredients lightly. Serve on bed of lettuce. (Makes an excellent sandwich for lunchbox toters.)

SEAFOOD MIXED GRILL

4 small lobster tails
6 giant shrimp
Small piece haddock or halibut
¼ pound bay scallops
Juice of 2 lemons
1 tablespoon minced parsley

Sprinkle first 4 items with lemon juice and minced parsley. Broil 5 minutes on each side.

FISH SALAD FINLANDIA

2 cups cold boiled
salmon, cod, or halibut,
cut into ½-inch cubes
1 celery heart, boiled,
chilled, cut into 1-inch
pieces
1 cup cooked sliced
mushrooms, chilled
1 teaspoon salt

½ teaspoon freshly
ground black pepper
1 tablespoon wine
vinegar
½ envelope artificial
sweetener, or equiva-
lent
1 tablespoon chopped
fresh parsley

Combine all ingredients and toss lightly. Serve on bed
of crisp lettuce leaves.

FISH ESPAGNOLE

Fillet of cod or haddock
1 package frozen chopped spinach
3 green peppers, chopped
1 cup cherry tomatoes
1 onion, sliced
Salt and pepper
¼ teaspoon garlic powder
¼ teaspoon orégano

Preheat oven to 375°. Sauté all vegetables and seasonings
except spinach in Teflon or waterless cooker. Put fish in
baking dish. Break frozen spinach in quarters and arrange
around fish. Pour rest of vegetables over. Bake 40 minutes.

BAKED CARP

1 piece carp	½ teaspoon salt
1 large onion, sliced thin	¼ teaspoon pepper
½ teaspoon paprika	1 tablespoon water
½ teaspoon garlic powder	

Preheat oven to 350°. Lay sliced onion in bottom of baking dish. Place fish on top. Make paste of remaining ingredients, and spread evenly on fish. Bake until fish appears dry.

TUNA SPREAD

1 can tuna, drained
¼ cup skim milk
Salt and pepper to taste

Blend all ingredients in blender and use as sandwich spread or serve mounded on lettuce with other salad vegetables.

FISH SCAMPI

½ pound shrimp	1 1-pound can tomatoes
½ pound scallops	1 tablespoon lemon juice
½ pound any kind fish fillet	½ teaspoon orégano
½ dozen clams (in shell)	1 teaspoon garlic powder
1 8-ounce can tomato sauce	Salt and pepper
1 cup juice from shrimp	1 1-pound can bean sprouts, heated

Cook and clean shrimp. Reserve 1 cup juice from cooking shrimp. Cut up shrimp, scallops, and fish fillet. Combine tomato sauce, shrimp juice, tomatoes, lemon juice, and sea-

sonings. Pour over cut-up fish mixture. Place clams on top.
Cover and simmer for 30 minutes. Pour over heated bean
sprouts.

ITALIAN TUNA AND PEPPERS

2 6½-ounce cans tuna,
drained
3 green peppers, cut in
thin slices
2 medium onions, sliced
¼ cup water
1 envelope chicken
bouillon, or 1 cube

½ teaspoon basil
1½ teaspoons salt
1 1-pound can tomatoes,
puréed in blender
¼ teaspoon Tabasco
sauce

Combine green peppers, onions, water, and chicken bouillon powder or cube. Cook until vegetables are tender. Add
basil, salt, tomatoes, and Tabasco. Simmer 10 minutes. Add
tuna. Heat.

HADDOCK AUX CHAMPIGNONS

Haddock fillets
1 small onion, sliced
½ pound mushrooms,
sliced
1 tablespoon chopped
parsley
1 clove garlic, minced
½ envelope chicken
bouillon powder

1 teaspoon salt
⅛ teaspoon freshly ground
pepper
½ cup skim milk
Juice of 1 lemon
⅛ cup grated Parmesan
cheese

Preheat oven to 350°. Sauté onions, mushrooms, parsley,
and garlic in tiny amount water with ½ envelope chicken
bouillon powder added. Stir in salt, pepper, and milk, and

heat. Place fish in baking dish. Sprinkle with lemon juice. Pour sauce over fish. Sprinkle evenly with cheese. Bake for 40 minutes.

POACHED HALIBUT STEAKS

2 pounds halibut steaks, 1″ thick
3 cups water
5 envelopes chicken bouillon or equivalent

Put fish in large skillet and add water, making sure fish is covered. Add 4 envelopes of the broth. Bring to boil. Cover and cook gently 10 minutes. Remove fish from liquid and sprinkle with remaining envelope broth powder.

TUNA MARINARA

1 can tuna, drained
1 can string beans, French style
1 can mushroom pieces
3 tablespoons prepared mustard
4 heaping tablespoons Marinara Sauce (See Index.)

Preheat oven to 350°. Mix all ingredients in casserole. Bake 1 hour.

SOUPS

Note: Try soup as a first course at Meal number 2 or Meal number 3. Soup takes the edge off your hunger and helps round out a meal. Large, satisfying meals of good food are the secret weapon that helps control cheating with junk foods. All soup recipes marked *Unlimited* can also be used in unlimited quantities at any time of the day or night for snacking.

PARSLEY-VEGETABLE BOUILLON

1 envelope vegetable bouillon powder, or equivalent
1 cup water, boiling
1 tablespoon finely chopped fresh parsley

Dissolve vegetable bouillon concentrate in one cup boiling water. Sprinkle parsley on top. *Unlimited*.

MADRILÈNE SOUP

1 envelope chicken bouillon powder, or equivalent
¼ cup finely slivered raw carrot
1 teaspoon minced onion
1½ cups water

Combine all ingredients in saucepan. Bring to boil. Simmer 5 minutes.

MUSHROOM SOUP

   1 envelope beef bouillon powder, or equivalent
1¼ cups water, boiling
   1 can mushroom slices and liquid

Dissolve bouillon concentrate in boiling water in saucepan. Add mushroom slices. Cook only until mushrooms are heated through. *Unlimited*.

VEGETABLE SOUP

   1 envelope beef bouillon powder, or equivalent
   1 cup water
  ½ cup mixed carrots and peas
  ¼ cup shredded cabbage
   1 stalk celery, diced
  ¼ cup tomato juice
   1 teaspoon minced onion
Salt and pepper to taste

Prepare vegetables and add to mixture of bouillon concentrate, water, and tomato juice. Simmer together for about 20 minutes. (This soup contains your ½ cup limited vegetable)

VEGETABLE BOUILLON

   1 envelope vegetable bouillon powder, or equivalent
   1 cup water
  ¼ cup chopped celery with tops
  ¼ cup chopped green pepper
   1 teaspoon dried onion flakes

Mix all ingredients in saucepan and simmer 10 minutes. *Unlimited*.

BEAN SPROUT SOUP

   2 envelopes chicken bouillon powder, or equivalent
   2 cups water
   1 can bean sprouts, including liquid
   ¼ cup chopped green pepper
   1 small can mushroom pieces, including liquid

Mix all ingredients in saucepan and simmer 10 minutes.
Unlimited.

CABBAGE SOUP

   2 envelopes onion bouillon powder, or equivalent
   2 cups water
   ¼ head cabbage, shredded fine

Mix all ingredients in saucepan and simmer 10 minutes.
Unlimited.

CREAM OF SPINACH SOUP

   1 package frozen chopped spinach
   2 envelopes chicken bouillon powder, or equivalent
   ⅓ cup powdered dry skim milk
   1 cup water
   ¼ teaspoon nutmeg
   ¼ teaspoon garlic salt

Mix all ingredients in blender and heat to boiling point,
stirring occasionally.

166

CREAM OF ASPARAGUS SOUP

Small can asparagus pieces, including liquid
1 envelope chicken bouillon, or equivalent
⅓ cup powdered dry skim milk
1 tablespoon chopped onion
¼ teaspoon nutmeg

Mix all ingredients in blender and heat.

TOMATO-CELERY SOUP

2 envelopes beef bouillon, or equivalent
2 cups water
1 cup tomato juice
1 cup finely chopped celery
¼ cup finely chopped onion
Salt and pepper

Simmer all ingredients in saucepan 10 minutes.

JELLIED CONSOMMÉ

1 envelope unflavored gelatin
2 cups water
2 envelopes beef bouillon, or equivalent
1 teaspoon parsley flakes
⅛ teaspoon freshly ground black pepper

Dissolve gelatin in ½ cup of the cold water. Heat remaining water to boiling, add bouillon concentrate, and pour into gelatin mixture. Add parsley flakes and pepper. Stir. Chill until set. Cut into cubes and serve in sherbet glasses or bouillon cups. (Excellent in hot weather.) *Unlimited*.

JELLIED CLAM-TOMATO SOUP

1 envelope unflavored gelatin
1¾ cups tomato juice
¾ cup clam juice
¼ teaspoon celery salt
2 tablespoons lemon juice
½ teaspoon Worcestershire sauce
⅛ teaspoon Tabasco sauce

Sprinkle gelatin in ½ cup of the tomato juice to soften. Place over low heat and stir until gelatin is dissolved. Remove from heat and add remaining tomato juice and all other ingredients. Pour into 8″ square pan and chill until firm. Cut into cubes and serve. Top each cube with a very thin lemon slice. (Excellent in hot weather.)

BEEF BORSCHT

1 quart water
1 pound very lean cubed beef
1 leek
1 onion, chopped
1 tomato, cut up small
½ carrot, sliced
1 teaspoon salt
1 pound cabbage, cored and shredded
1 tablespoon lemon juice
1 teaspoon artificial sweetener or equivalent

Heat water to boiling. Add beef, leek, onion, tomato, carrot, and salt. Cover and simmer slowly for 2 hours. Remove beef. Add cabbage. Cook 10 minutes. Add lemon and artificial sweetener. Return meat and bring to boiling point. Serve. (This is a main-dish soup.)

CLAM CHOWDER MANHATTAN

2 cups water
2 envelopes beef bouillon powder, or 2 cubes
½ cup tomato juice
2 tablespoons minced onion
1 large stalk celery, chopped
1 teaspoon thyme
1 8-ounce can minced clams and juice

Simmer all ingredients for 20 minutes. (This is a main-dish soup.)

ONION SOUP

3 thinly sliced white onions
1 small bay leaf
1 teaspoon chopped fresh parsley
2 cups hot water
1 envelope chicken bouillon powder, or 1 cube
½ teaspoon Kitchen Bouquet

1 teaspoon Worcestershire sauce
2 drops liquid artificial sweetener or equivalent
Sprinkle of freshly ground black pepper
1 teaspoon grated Parmesan cheese

Cook onions in heavy skillet without adding any fat. Stir and turn onions constantly until lightly browned. Add bay leaf, parsley, hot water, chicken bouillon concentrate, Kitchen Bouquet, and Worcestershire sauce. Bring to boil. Lower heat and simmer ½ hour. Add artificial sweetener and pepper to taste. Sprinkle with grated cheese.

RUBY CONSOMMÉ

1 cup tomato juice
1 envelope chicken bouillon
    powder, or 1 cube
1 bay leaf

2 peppercorns, whole
Salt and pepper
Lemon slices

Mix all ingredients except lemon and simmer 15 minutes. Strain out bay leaf and peppercorns. Float a thin slice of lemon on each serving.

GAZPACHO

1 small onion, chopped
½ clove garlic, minced
1 green pepper, chopped
1 small tomato, chopped
⅛ teaspoon freshly
    ground black pepper

½ teaspoon Spanish
    paprika
⅛ cup wine vinegar
¾ cup cold water
½ cucumber, peeled and
    thinly sliced

Combine all ingredients except wine vinegar, water, and cucumber. Blend in blender until a purée. Chill 2 hours in glass or plastic bowl (not metal). Add cucumber slices, vinegar and water just before serving. (Excellent in hot weather.)

CHICKEN SOUP WITH "DUMPLINGS"

5 cups cold water
½ teaspoon salt
3 envelopes chicken
    bouillon powder, or 3
    cubes
2 stalks celery, sliced
1 large carrot, peeled
    and sliced

4 large fresh mush-
    rooms, sliced
10 fresh cauliflower
    buds broken into
    smaller buds

Put water and salt in soup pot and bring to boil. Add chicken bouillon concentrate. Add celery, carrot, and mushrooms. Simmer 15 minutes. Add cauliflower buds and simmer 10 minutes longer.

LEFTOVER-BROCCOLI SOUP

Leftover broccoli
Water
1 envelope onion bouillon powder, or equivalent
Salt and pepper to taste

Put broccoli in blender with enough water to purée. Place purée in saucepan with onion bouillon concentrate, salt, and pepper. Heat and serve. *Unlimited.*

INSTANT VEGETABLE SOUP

1 envelope beef bouillon powder, or 1 cube
1 envelope onion bouillon, or equivalent
3 cups water
4 heaping tablespoons Ehler's Dehydrated Vegetables (or any brand without potatoes).

Mix all ingredients in saucepan. Simmer 15 minutes. *Unlimited.*

HUNGARIAN CAULIFLOWER SOUP

2 envelopes chicken bouillon, or 2 cubes
2 cups water
2 medium carrots, sliced
1 package frozen cauliflower
¼ cup skim milk
Salt and pepper to taste

Combine bouillon concentrate, water, carrots, and cauliflower. Cook until carrots are tender. Stir in skim milk. Add salt and pepper.

CREAM OF CELERY SOUP

3 stalks celery, cut up
1 envelope chicken bouillon, or 1 cube
⅓ cup skim milk powder
⅓ cup water

Blend all ingredients in blender. Bring to boiling point. Serve.

BEEF

Note: Beef is the most popular American meat. It is, however, rather high in calories. We suggest care in menu planning to avoid winding up a week of otherwise good eating with 7 beef dinners in a row. Be sure to vary beef meals with poultry, lamb, fish, and veal.

BEEF AND PEPPERS

1½ pounds very lean stew beef
1 envelope onion bouillon powder, or 1 cube
½ cup water
1 onion, chopped
2 green peppers, cut up
1 cup tomatoes (preferably fresh), cut up
½ teaspoon orégano
½ teaspoon garlic salt

Dissolve onion bouillon powder in water. Add beef and onions and brown. Add vegetables and seasonings. Simmer 1½ hours.

BEEF STEW

1 very lean flank steak
1 1-pound can tomatoes (put through blender)
2 envelopes onion bouillon powder, or equivalent
1 green pepper, sliced
1 small can mushrooms or 6 fresh mushrooms, sliced
1 teaspoon basil
2 packages frozen French-style string beans

Broil flank steak. Cut in diagonal strips. Bring tomatoes, bouillon, peppers, mushrooms, and basil to boil. Add sliced steak and simmer 1½ hours. Add string beans. Cook another 15 minutes.

MEAT LOAF

2 pounds lean chopped beef
1 egg
1 small onion, grated
½ teaspoon garlic salt
⅛ teaspoon pepper
1 teaspoon Worcestershire sauce

Preheat oven to 350°. Mix all ingredients thoroughly. Bake in loaf pan for 1 hour. If desired, pour small amount of tomato juice over the loaf before baking.

MUSHROOM MEAT LOAF

Same as the above basic meat loaf recipe, with the addition of 1 can of drained mushroom pieces.

CREOLE MEATBALLS

Basic meat loaf recipe
2 green peppers, thinly sliced
1 onion, thinly sliced
3 stalks celery, cut up
1 1-pound can tomatoes
½ teaspoon basil
Salt and pepper

Preheat oven to 350°. Using basic meat loaf ingredients, form small meatballs. Brown in heavy skillet. Pour off any excess fat that forms in pan during browning. Place meatballs in casserole. Add cut-up vegetables and seasonings. Pour can of tomatoes over all. Bake for 1¼ hours.

STUFFED PEPPERS

Basic meat loaf recipe
1 tablespoon grated Parmesan cheese
4 large green peppers
1 cup Marinara Sauce (See Index.)

Preheat oven to 350°. Add cheese to basic meat loaf recipe. Cut peppers in half and stuff with meat mixture. Pour Marinara Sauce over them. Bake 1 hour.

MEATBALLS MARINARA

Basic meat loaf recipe
1 teaspoon orégano
1 cup Marinara Sauce (See Index.)

Add orégano to basic meat loaf recipe. Form in small balls and brown in heavy skillet. Pour off any excess fat that forms in pan during browning. Pour Marinara Sauce over and simmer about ¾ hour.

SCRAMBLED HAMBURG

1 pound very lean chopped beef
1 can mushroom pieces, drained
1 stalk celery, finely diced
1 tiny onion, chopped
1 green pepper, chopped
Salt and pepper

Combine all ingredients and brown slowly in heavy skillet.

CHINESE PEPPER STEAK

1 pound top or bottom round steak, thinly sliced
¼ cup soy sauce
1 envelope artificial sweetener, or equivalent
1 clove garlic, minced
¼ teaspoon ginger
1 green pepper, cut up
1 large tomato, cut up

Marinate meat strips in soy sauce and artificial sweetener for ½ hour. Brown garlic and ginger in heavy skillet, stirring constantly. Add peppers and brown 3 minutes. Add meat and juices and brown 3 minutes. Add tomato and cook 3 minutes. (Delicious served over a bed of bean sprouts.)

SWEDISH MEATBALLS

1 pound ground round steak
1 onion, diced fine
1 teaspoon nutmeg
Salt and pepper
1 cup water
2 envelopes beef bouillon powder, or equivalent

Cook onion in tiny amount water until soft. Add to meat and seasonings in bowl and mix well. Form tiny balls. Brown in heavy skillet. Mix beef bouillon concentrate with water and pour over meatballs. Simmer ½ hour.

HORSERADISH BEEF BAKE

1 pound lean round steak, cut in 1″ squares
1 onion, chopped
2 envelopes beef bouillon powder, or equivalent
2 cups water, boiling
3 tablespoons horseradish
Salt and pepper

Preheat oven to 300°. Place beef squares in casserole. Mix all other ingredients and pour over beef. Bake 2½ hours.

GERMAN FRANKFURTERS

1 pound frankfurters (all beef)
2 cups sauerkraut
1 small diced onion
2 envelopes beef bouillon powder, or equivalent
1 envelope artificial sweetener, or equivalent
1 cup water
½ teaspoon caraway seeds
Salt and pepper

Combine all ingredients and simmer about 30 minutes in covered pot.

CONEY ISLAND HOT DOGS

1 pound frankfurters (all beef)
1 green pepper, minced
1 onion, minced
1 evelope onion bouillon powder, or 1 cube
¼ cup water

Sauté peppers and onions slowly in water and onion bouillon concentrate until liquid is absorbed. Broil frankfurters, turning frequently. When almost done, remove and slit each frankfurter. Stuff with vegetable mixture. Return and broil a few minutes longer.

KNOCKWURST SUPREME

4 knockwurst (all beef)
1 1-pound can tomatoes
1 onion, sliced thin
1 teaspoon basil
1 tablespoon grated Cheddar cheese

Preheat oven to 350°. Cut knockwurst in diagonal 1″ slices. Place in baking dish with tomatoes, onion, and basil. Bake for 1 hour. Just before baking time is up, sprinkle with grated cheese.

ITALIAN CASSEROLE

1 pound lean chopped beef
1 cup cubed eggplant
1 sliced green pepper
1 sliced zucchini squash
4 large mushrooms, sliced
1 teaspoon onion flakes
½ teaspoon orégano
¼ teaspoon garlic powder
Salt and pepper
1 8-ounce can tomato sauce
1 teaspoon grated Parmesan cheese

Preheat oven to 350°. Brown all vegetables in heavy skillet. Brown beef in heavy skillet. Mix all together in casserole, adding seasonings. Pour tomato sauce over and sprinkle with grated cheese. Bake ½ hour.

CHILE

1½ pounds lean ground beef
1 cup chopped green pepper
½ cup chopped onion
1 8-ounce can tomato sauce
1 clove garlic, minced
3 teaspoons chili powder
Salt and pepper
1 envelope onion bouillon powder, or equivalent

Mix all ingredients and simmer 1½ hours. (Excellent to freeze for use at a later date.)

LIVERBURGER

1 pound calves' liver
1 minced onion
1 minced green pepper
½ teaspoon garlic powder
Salt and pepper

Put liver through meat grinder. Add all other ingredients and mix thoroughly. Form into burgers. Broil.

LIVER WITH BRAISED ONIONS

1 pound calves' liver
½ cup water
1 envelope beef bouillon powder, or 1 cube
Dash Worcestershire sauce
Salt and pepper
1 onion, sliced thin

Put water, beef bouillon concentrate, Worcestershire sauce, salt, and pepper in heavy skillet. Add sliced onions. Braise slowly until liquid is almost absorbed. Broil liver. When liver is nearly done, spoon braised onions on top of each slice and broil 3 minutes longer.

BEEF SHISH KEBAB

Marinade: ¾ cup vinegar
¾ cup water
2 bay leaves
1 teaspoon salt
1 envelope artificial sweetener, or equivalent

Combine all ingredients. Bring to boil. Simmer 5 minutes. Cool.

1½ pounds very lean round steak, cut in cubes
Whole mushrooms
Whole tiny peeled pearl onions
Green pepper cut in squares
Cherry tomatoes

Pour cooled marinade over beef cubes. Let stand 24 hours. Drain, but reserve marinade juices. Alternate meat and vegetables on skewers. Broil, turning frequently, basting often with reserved marinade.

STUFFED MUSHROOMS MARIA

1 pound very lean chopped beef
Salt and pepper
½ teaspoon garlic powder
Very large fresh mushrooms
¼ cup tomato juice
2 tablespoons chopped parsley

Preheat oven to 350°. Mix beef with salt, pepper, and garlic powder. Mound into large mushroom caps. (Save the mushroom stems for use in another dish.) Pour thin layer of tomato juice on cookie sheet. Set stuffed mushroom caps in this. Sprinkle with remaining tomato juice and chopped parsley. Bake ½ hour.

SWEET AND SOUR BEEF

1 pound leftover roast beef sliced
2 teaspoons horseradish
2 teaspoons prepared mustard
1 teaspoon grated onion
2 teaspoons vinegar
1 envelope artificial sweetener, or equivalent
Salt and pepper
¼ cup hot water

Brown meat slices lightly in heavy skillet. Add remaining ingredients. Cover. Simmer 20 minutes.

STUFFED FLANK STEAK

1 very lean flank steak
1 onion, chopped
1 green pepper, chopped
1 can mushroom slices
¼ teaspoon rosemary
Salt and pepper

Cut all visible fat from flank steak and spread out flat. Mix raw vegetables and seasonings and spread this mixture over surface of flank steak. Roll tightly and tie or skewer. Brown well in heavy skillet, turning roll frequently. Lower heat. Add a little water. Cover and simmer for 1½ to 2 hours, depending on size of flank steak. If pan appears too dry, add a little more water. To serve, slice across roll.

SWISS STEAK

1 pound lean round steak
Salt and pepper to taste
1 small onion, chopped
2 stalks celery, chopped
2 cloves garlic, crushed
1 tablespoon A-1 Sauce
1 can tomatoes

Sprinkle meat with salt and pepper. Brown well on both sides. Add onion, celery, and garlic, and sauté until onion is soft. Add remaining ingredients. Cover and simmer 1½ hours, or until meat is tender.

DEVILED SWISS STEAK

1 pound very lean round steak
1 8-ounce can tomatoes, sieved
1 teaspoon prepared mustard
1 tablespoon soy sauce
1 tablespoon parsley flakes
½ teapsoon salt
⅛ teaspoon pepper
1 onion, sliced
1 large carrot, sliced

Brown meat in heavy skillet. Add tomatoes and all seasonings. Cover tightly. Simmer 2 hours. During last 30 minutes, add onion and carrot.

CHOP SUEY

1 pound ground round steak
1 can Chinese vegetables
1 can sliced mushrooms
½ cup sliced water chestnuts
1 teaspoon soy sauce
Salt and pepper

Brown meat in heavy skillet. Drain any excess fat that forms in pan. Add drained Chinese vegetables, mushrooms, and water chestnuts. Cover to heat vegetables. Add soy sauce, salt, and pepper. Serve.

SKILLET SUPPER

½ cup chopped onion
1 clove garlic, minced
1 whole clove
1 pound all beef franks cut in 1″ pieces
2 tablespoons capers
1 tablespoon vinegar

1 whole fresh tomato, diced
1 head cabbage, finely shredded
Freshly ground black pepper
¼ cup water

Cook onion, garlic, and whole clove in tiny amount of water in large heavy skillet until onion is soft. Add diced franks, capers, vinegar, diced tomato, and shredded cabbage. Stir well. Sprinkle with pepper. Add the water. Cover. Simmer 15 minutes.

CHILI BURGERS

1½ pounds very lean ground beef
1 teaspoon salt
¼ teaspoon pepper
1 1-pound can tomatoes (drain but reserve juice)
1 clove garlic, minced fine
1 scant teaspoon chili powder

Mix beef with salt and pepper and shape into small hamburgers. Brown well on both sides in heavy skillet. Remove. Add drained tomatoes, garlic, and chili powder and cook in same pan 2 minutes. Add ½ cup reserved juice from tomatoes, and hamburger patties. Simmer 15 minutes, basting frequently with sauce in pan.

PIZZA BEEF

½ pound lean ground beef
2 tablespoons skim milk powder
Salt and pepper
¼ teaspoon garlic powder

½ small onion, grated
½ teaspoon Worcestershire sauce
1 8-ounce can tomato sauce
2 very thin slices Provolone cheese

Preheat oven to 350°. Mix beef, skim milk powder, salt, pepper, garlic powder, grated onion, and Worcestershire sauce. Line a small pie plate with this mixture. Bake until well done. Pour off any accumulated fat that may appear. Pour tomato sauce over and top with cheese. Return to oven until cheese is melted and bubbly. (Note: Meal number 2 only.)

STUFFED CABBAGE

8 to 10 large cabbage leaves
1 pound lean chopped beef
1 small onion, grated
Salt and pepper
½ teaspoon garlic powder

1 teaspoon soy sauce
1 teaspoon Worcestershire sauce
1 1-pound can tomatoes
1 teaspoon caraway seeds

Preheat oven to 350°. Place cabbage leaves in boiling water until tender enough to fold. Mix beef, onion, salt, pepper, garlic powder, soy sauce, and Worcestershire sauce. Place a spoonful of this mixture in the center of each cabbage leaf and fold into bundles. Pour tomatoes over. Sprinkle evenly with caraway seeds. Bake 1 hour, turning and basting bundles occasionally.

SUKIYAKI

1 pound beef, sliced very thin (chicken, veal, or liver
can also be used)
1 package frozen Japanese vegetables
1 tablespoon soy sauce

Brown meat thoroughly. Remove sauce cubes from frozen
vegetables and discard. Add plain vegetables to browned
meat. Add soy sauce. Cover and bring to boiling point.
Serve.

MARINATED RIB STEAK

2 rib steaks
½ cup soy sauce
½ teaspoon garlic powder
1½ envelopes artificial sweetener, or equivalent
1 teaspoon ground ginger
¼ teaspoon black pepper

Combine soy sauce, garlic powder, sweetener, ginger, and
pepper. Marinate rib steaks in this mixture for 2 hours,
turning frequently. Broil 8 minutes on each side, brushing
occasionally with reserved marinade mixture.

TANGY MARINATED BEEF

2½ pounds lean round steak	½ teaspoon salt
1 cup vinegar	10 whole peppercorns
2 onions, chopped	⅛ teaspoon ground cloves
2 large carrots, sliced	3 bay leaves

Put beef in flat pan. Combine all other ingredients and
bring to boil. Pour over meat. Cover and refrigerate for 2

days, turning meat occasionally. Brown meat on all sides. Add marinade. Cover and simmer about 1½ hours.

BEEF JAPONAIS

1 pound lean round steak cut in strips
1 cup chopped onion
1 package frozen French-style string beans
2 chicken bouillon cubes dissolved in 1 cup boiling water
¼ teaspoon ginger
1 tablespoon soy sauce
1 teaspoon salt
1 cup sliced green pepper
2 large stalks celery, cut up
1 large fresh tomato cut in small wedges

Brown meat. Add onion, string beans, bouillon, ginger, soy sauce, and salt. Simmer until string beans are almost tender. Add green pepper, celery, and tomato. Simmer 10 to 15 minutes longer.

UNSTUFFED CABBAGE

1 head cabbage, cut up
1 apple, pared and sliced
1 pound lean chopped beef
1 8-ounce can tomato sauce
1 tablespoon lemon juice
½ envelope artificial sweetener, or equivalent

Steam cabbage until almost soft. Drain. Add apples and cook 10 minutes. Brown chopped meat and add to cabbage and apples. Add tomato sauce, lemon juice, and sweetener. Cover and simmer until apples and cabbage are very soft. (Freezes well.)

FRENCH STEW

1 pound lean chopped beef
½ pound mushrooms, sliced
1 carrot, sliced
½ head cauliflower, cut in buds
1 envelope beef bouillon, or 1 cube
Water
Salt and pepper

Brown beef. Place all ingredients in saucepan. Add water to cover. Bring to boil and simmer until tender. Drain off liquid.

VEAL

VEAL CARIOCA

1 pound ground veal
1 small onion, chopped
½ teaspoon garlic salt
Pepper
1 chopped green pepper
1 cup tomato juice

Mix ground veal with ½ the onion, garlic salt, and pepper. Form into balls. Brown in heavy skillet. Add chopped green pepper and remaining onion. Cover with tomato juice. Cover. Simmer 45 minutes.

VEAL ROLLS

1 pound Italian-style veal cutlets
1 can sliced mushrooms (drain liquid and reserve.)
1 stalk celery, chopped
1 green pepper, chopped
¼ teaspoon poultry seasoning
Salt and pepper

Spread cutlets flat. Mix all other ingredients except liquid from mushrooms. Place some of this mixture in the center of each cutlet. Roll and tie. Brown in heavy skillet. Add liquid from mushrooms. Cover and simmer about 1 hour.

VEAL AND PEPPERS

1 pound veal cut in pieces
1 onion, cut up
1 green pepper, cut up
1 clove garlic, minced
1 teaspoon paprika
1 tomato, cut up

Brown veal in heavy skillet. Set aside. Brown onion and green pepper and season with garlic and paprika. Add cut up tomato. Simmer gently for few minutes. Add veal, cook 45 minutes longer.

VEALBURGERS

1 pound ground veal
1 small onion, minced
½ teaspoon seasoned salt
4 large fresh mushrooms, sliced

Mix veal, onion, and seasoned salt. Form patties. Broil. During last few minutes of broiling, cover tops of patties with mushroom slices.

BRAISED VEAL CHOPS

4 veal chops
2 small onions, sliced
Salt and pepper
Water to cover

Put all ingredients in heavy frying pan. Cover. Simmer 1½ hours, turning chops when browned on one side.

VEAL STEW

1½ pounds lean veal cubes
1 envelope vegetable bouillon powder, or 1 cube
1 cup water
1 cup tomato juice
½ onion, minced
1 clove garlic
1 bay leaf

Salt
Pepper
6 large mushrooms, sliced
3 stalks celery and leaves, sliced
1 package frozen French-style string beans
2 carrots, sliced

Bring first nine ingredients to boil. Cover and simmer 1 hour. Add remaining ingredients and cook another ½ hour.

VEAL-STUFFED MUSHROOMS

1 pound lean chopped veal
Salt and pepper
½ teaspoon garlic powder
Very large fresh mushrooms
¼ cup tomato juice
2 tablespoons chopped parsley

Preheat oven to 350°. Mix veal with salt, pepper, and garlic powder. Mound into mushroom caps. (Save mushroom stems for use in another dish.)

Pour thin layer tomato juice on cookie sheet. Set stuffed caps in this. Sprinkle with tomato juice and chopped parsley. Bake ½ hour.

VEAL MOZZARELLA

1½ pounds Italian-style veal cutlets
1 envelope onion bouillon powder, or equivalent
¼ cup water
Salt and pepper
A few very thin slices Mozzarella cheese
1 cup Marinara Sauce (See Index.)

Preheat oven to 350°. Mix onion bouillon concentrate, water, and salt and pepper. Brown veal in this mixture in heavy frying pan until liquid is absorbed. Place cutlets in baking dish. Lay thin slices of cheese on top of meat. Add Marinara Sauce. Bake ½ hour.

VEAL SAVORY

    1 pound veal cutlet cut in 2″ pieces
⅛ cup water
    1 tablespoon vinegar
½ teaspoon salt
½ teaspoon paprika
    1 bay leaf
    1 clove garlic, mashed
    1 cup canned tomatoes
    1 envelope artificial sweetener, or equivalent

Make a marinade of water, vinegar, salt, paprika, bay leaf, and garlic. Mix well and pour over meat in shallow pan. Let stand 4 hours, turning occasionally. Drain, and save liquid. Brown meat in heavy skillet. Add tomatoes, artificial sweetener, and reserved marinade liquid. Cover. Simmer 1 hour.

BAKED VEAL LOAF

1¼ pounds choppd veal
    1 onion, chopped
    2 tablespoons pimiento, minced
    1 green pepper, chopped
    2 tablespoons skim milk powder
    1 tablespoon lemon juice
    1 egg, beaten
Salt and pepper
    1 teaspoon paprika
½ cup beef bouillon

Preheat oven to 325°. Combine all ingredients except beef bouillon. Shape into loaf. Bake 2 hours. After first half hour, pour beef bouillon over and baste frequently.

VEAL AND BROCCOLI CASSEROLE

2 veal patties broken in half
1 box frozen broccoli
½ onion, diced fine
2 ounces canned mixed vegetable juice
Jane's Crazy Mixed-Up Salt
   (A spice available in your market, hopefully)

Preheat oven to 350°. Combine all ingredients in a covered casserole. Bake about 40 minutes.

CURRIED VEAL CHOPS

4 veal chops
¾ cup chopped onion
2 to 3 tablespoons curry powder
1½ teaspoon salt
¼ teaspoon seasoned salt
Freshly ground black pepper
¼ cup water
1 red apple
Lemon juice

Trim all fat from chops and brown them. Spoon onion around chops. Sauté. Sprinkle with all spices and seasonings. Add water. Cover. Cook 45 minutes over medium heat. Core apple, leaving skin on, and cut up. Brush apple pieces with lemon juice and place around chops. Cover. Cook 15 minutes longer.

VEAL CHOP SUEY

1 pound lean cubed veal
2 tablespoons hot water
1 cup diced celery
½ cup diced green
pepper
½ cup diced onion
1 teaspoon salt

⅛ teaspoon pepper
1½ teaspoons soy sauce
1 envelope beef bouillon
powder, or equivalent
1 cup hot water
Bean sprouts

Brown veal in heavy skillet. Add 2 tablespoons hot water. Cover and simmer 5 minutes. Add remaining ingredients. Cover and simmer 40 minutes. Serve over heated bean sprouts.

VEAL BALLS

2 pounds chopped veal
2 tablespoons onion flakes
2 eggs
1 green pepper, chopped
Salt and pepper
24 ounces tomato juice

Mix veal, onion flakes, eggs, green pepper, and salt and pepper to taste. Form small balls and add to simmering tomato juice. Cook about 20 minutes.

LAMB

LAMB CHOP GRILL

Baby rib lamb chops
Salt and pepper
1 fresh tomato, cut in half
1 teaspoon grated American cheese

Season chops with salt and pepper. Broil. Just before chops are done, top each tomato half with grated cheese and salt and pepper and broil.

ROAST LEG OF LAMB WITH GARLIC

Leg of lamb
2 cloves garlic, cut up
Salt and pepper

Preheat oven to 350°. Make tiny slits in leg of lamb. Stuff slits with bits of garlic clove. Season with salt and pepper. Roast 1½ hours or until lamb is very well done.

LAMB STEW

4 shoulder lamb chops, all fat cut off
1 1-pound can tomatoes
1 onion, sliced
2 large celery stalks, cut in large diagonal pieces
½ teaspoon garlic powder
⅛ teaspoon basil
Salt and pepper

Brown chops in heavy skillet. Add all other ingredients and simmer slowly 1½ hours.

BRAISED LAMB CHOPS

4 shoulder lamb chops, all fat cut off
1 large onion, sliced
Salt and pepper
Water to cover

Put all ingredients in heavy frying pan. Cover and simmer about 1½ hours, turning chops when brown on one side.

LAMB PATTIES

1 pound lamb patties (available at butcher's or
    have butcher grind lamb.)
Salt and pepper
1 teaspoon minced parsley

Season patties with salt and pepper. Broil. Sprinkle with minced parsley. Serve.

GOURMET LAMB CHOPS

4 loin lamb chops, 1″ thick
Salt and pepper
4 slices Bermuda onion
8 tablespoons cottage cheese

Preheat oven to 375°. Wrap tail end of each chop around thick part to form a flat round patty; fasten with toothpicks. Sprinkle with salt and pepper. Place chops in shallow baking pan. Place one slice onion on each chop. Put 2 tablespoons cottage cheese on each chop. Add no water and do not cover. Bake for one hour.

IRISH STEW

2 pounds lamb cut in small pieces
Water to cover
3 allspice berries
2 tablespoons minced parsley
½ cup sliced carrots
½ cup diced turnips
½ cup sliced parsnips
½ cup sliced onion
Salt and pepper

Place meat in Dutch oven; add water to cover. Add all-spice berries and minced parsley. Cover and simmer for 2 hours. Add vegetables, salt, and pepper. Cook 45 minutes longer.

LAMB JULIENNE

1 pound boneless lamb shoulder, cut in 3″ strips
1 teaspoon salt
¼ teaspoon ground cloves
¼ cup water
½ pound fresh mushrooms, sliced
¾ cup milk (skim)
1 can bean sprouts

Brown lamb strips in heavy skillet. Add salt, cloves, and water. Cover. Cook over low heat 1 hour. Add mushrooms. Cook 15 minutes longer. Add milk. Cook 5 minutes. Serve over bed of bean sprouts.

LAMB RIBLETS WITH VEGETABLES

    2 pounds breast of lamb, cut into riblets
    1½ teaspoons salt
    ⅛ teaspoon pepper
    1 cup water
    6 small white pearl onions
    6 whole carrots
    ¾ pound whole green beans
    ¼ cup vinegar

Brown lamb on all sides in heavy skillet. Add salt, pepper, and water. Cover. Simmer 45 minutes. Add vegetables and cook 30 minutes longer. Add vinegar and cook 30 minutes longer.

LAMB CHOPS CREOLE

    6 shoulder lamb chops, fat removed
    1 medium onion, diced
    ½ cup diced green pepper
    2½ cups canned tomatoes, well drained
    ⅛ teaspoon cayenne pepper
    1 teaspoon salt
    ⅛ teaspoon chili powder

Preheat oven to 350°. Brown chops on both sides. Remove to casserole. Place onion and green pepper in skillet in which chops were browned and brown them lightly. Add tomatoes and seasonings. Stir and simmer for a few minutes. Pour mixture over chops. Cover tightly and bake for one hour.

BARBECUED LAMB RIBLETS

    2 pounds lamb riblets, fat removed
    1 cup wine vinegar
    3 to 4 envelopes artificial sweetener, or equivalent
    ¼ teaspoon salt
    ¼ teaspoon pepper
    2 tablespoons frozen orange juice concentrate
    ½ teaspoon garlic powder

Preheat oven to 350°. Mix all ingredients and marinate riblets in mixture for 2 to 3 hours. Bake on rack until deep brown, basting occasionally with marinade mixture.

DOLMAS

    1 pound lean ground lamb
    2 medium eggplants
    ½ cup diced onion
    1 8-ounce can tomato sauce
    2 tablespoons chopped parsley
    ½ teaspoon chopped mint
    ½ teaspoon chopped dill
    Salt and pepper
    1 fresh tomato

Preheat oven to 350°. Slice eggplant in half lengthwise. Scoop out and reserve insides, leaving shell intact. Sauté lamb and onions until lightly browned. Drain off fat. Chop eggplant pulp and add. Stir in tomato sauce and cook 10 minutes. Add all seasonings. Stuff eggplant shells with this mixture. Set in baking dish in ¼ inch water. Cover with aluminum foil. Bake for 50 minutes. Remove foil. Put fresh tomato slice on top and heat in broiler for 2 to 3 minutes.

SHISH KEBAB

¾ cup vinegar   2 bay leaves
¾ cup water   1 teaspoon salt
  1 envelope sweetener, or equivalent

Combine all ingredients. Bring to boil. Simmer 5 minutes. Cool and reserve.

1½ pounds lean lamb cubes
Fresh tomato cut in small wedges
Whole mushrooms
Pearl onions
Green pepper cubes

Poor cooled marinade over lamb cubes. Let stand 24 hours in refrigerator. Drain, but reserve marinade. Alternate lamb and vegetables on skewers. Broil, turning frequently and basting with marinade.

POULTRY

ROAST ROCK CORNISH GAME HEN

1 hen per person
Mushroom Stuffing (See Index.)

Preheat oven to 350°. Stuff each hen with a few table-spoons Mushroom Stuffing. Roast uncovered for about 1 hour.

TROPICAL CHICKEN

1 broiling chicken, cut up
¼ teaspoon garlic powder
Salt and pepper
4 celery stalks
¾ cup orange juice
Orange peel cut into strips
¼ teaspoon rosemary

Preheat oven to 325°. Rub chicken well with garlic powder, salt, and pepper. Place in baking dish over the stalks of celery. Pour orange juice over chicken and lay strips of orange peel on top of each piece. Sprinkle with rosemary. Bake for 1 hour.

LEMON CHICKEN

4 whole chicken breasts, skinned
1 tablespoon dry Italian seasoning
Salt and pepper
1 teaspoon garlic powder
1 teaspoon parsley flakes
¼ cup lemon juice

Combine seasonings and lemon juice. Wash and dry chicken and place in broiling pan, rib side up. Pour sauce over chicken. Broil 20 minutes, basting frequently with juices from pan. Turn. Broil 20 minutes, continuing to baste.

CHICKEN PIZZACANTE

1 pound chicken breasts or cutlets, cut in small pieces
Salt and pepper
1 envelope chicken bouillon powder, or equivalent
2 cloves fresh garlic, minced
3 tablespoons minced fresh parsley
1 bay leaf
Juice of 2 lemons
½ cup water

Sprinkle chicken with salt, pepper, and the bouillon concentrate. Sauté in heavy skillet until slightly browned. Add minced garlic, parsley, and bay leaf. Stir well. Add lemon juice and water. Simmer 45 minutes.

CHICKEN ITALIANO

4 chicken breasts
Juice of 1 lemon
Salt and pepper
1 teaspoon garlic powder
1 tablespoon orégano

Mix lemon juice, salt, pepper, garlic powder, and orégano. Rub thoroughly into chicken. Broil.

BAKED CHICKEN PARTS

1 broiler, cut up
1 can mushroom pieces
2 envelopes chicken bouillon powder
Salt and pepper

Preheat oven to 350°. Place chicken in baking dish. Pour can of mushrooms over it, including juice. Sprinkle with chicken bouillon powder, salt, and pepper. Bake for 1½ hours.

CHICKEN CACCIATORE

Chicken cutlets, cut in 2" pieces
½ pound fresh mushrooms, sliced
1 cup Marinara Sauce (See Index.)

Brown chicken pieces in heavy skillet. Add mushrooms and marinara sauce. Simmer 45 minutes.

CHICKEN SALAD DELIGHT

2 cups cubed cooked chicken
2 tablespoons shredded Cheddar cheese
1 cup chopped celery
½ cup chopped green pepper

Toss all ingredients lightly. Pour dressing over them. Toss again.

Dressing: 2 tablespoons vinegar
1 tablespoon mustard
⅛ cup water

CHICKEN OMELET

3 tablespoons diced cooked chicken
1 tablespoon minced onion
¼ cup chopped green pepper
1 egg
Salt and pepper
1 tablespoon skim milk

Sauté onion and green pepper in tiny amount of water until vegetables are tender. Add diced chicken. Cook 2 minutes. Add egg beaten with skim milk, salt, and pepper. Cover and cook until set. Turn over and finish cooking. (Meal number 2 only.)

CHICKEN WITH MUSHROOMS

4 chicken breasts, boned and cut in 2″ pieces
2 envelopes chicken bouillon powder, or equivalent
¼ cup water
1 pound fresh mushrooms, sliced thin
¼ teaspoon paprika
1 teaspoon salt
¼ teaspoon black pepper
½ teaspoon Worcestershire sauce

Mix chicken bouillon concentrate with water. Cook chicken pieces in about 2 tablespoons of this mixture until chicken is tender, stirring and turning constantly. Add mushrooms. Add remaining chicken bouillon mixture. Add paprika, salt, pepper, and Worcestershire sauce. Cook 5 minutes. Serve.

BARBECUED CHICKEN CHINOISE

1 chicken, cut up
⅓ cup soy sauce
¼ teaspoon garlic powder
½ teaspoon powdered mustard
¼ teaspoon ginger

Preheat oven to 350°. Lay chicken pieces in baking dish. Mix soy sauce, garlic powder, mustard, and ginger, and use mixture to baste chicken every 15 minutes, while it roasts for 1 hour.

SAUCE FOR BARBECUED CHICKEN CHINOISE

1 tablespoon powdered mustard
Enough water to make paste

Mix. Let stand 10 minutes. Dip chicken in while eating.

CHICKEN PIQUANT

1 broiling chicken, cut up
½ cup chicken bouillon
3 tablespoons vinegar
¼ teaspoon dry mustard
½ teaspoon salt
¼ teaspoon pepper
¼ teaspoon paprika
1 clove garlic, minced fine

Place chicken pieces in shallow pan. Combine all other ingredients. Pour over chicken. Let stand in refrigerator 1 hour, turning chicken once. Remove and broil chicken pieces, basting frequently with reserved marinade.

ARABIAN CHICKEN

1 chicken, cut up
1 small onion, chopped
1 clove garlic, minced
1 small eggplant, cut up
1 green pepper, sliced thin
½ teaspoon allspice
1 small can sliced mushrooms, drained
1 1-pound can tomatoes
1 teaspoon salt
¼ teaspoon pepper
2 bay leaves
½ teaspoon thyme

Preheat oven to 350°. Brown chicken pieces in heavy skillet without added fat. Remove to baking dish. Place onion, garlic, eggplant, and green pepper in same skillet and sauté over low heat for 10 minutes. Spoon over chicken. Mix and add all remaining ingredients. Cover. Bake for 30 minutes. Remove cover. Bake 30 minutes longer.

"FRIED" CHICKEN

1 2½-pound broiler cut in pieces
1 cup chicken bouillon

Preheat oven to 400°. Rinse the pieces of a 2½ pound broiler in cold water and dry. Pour ½ cup of the chicken bouillon into shallow pan. Lay chicken pieces skin side down in this broth. Bake at 400° for 30 minutes. Turn chicken and add the other ½ cup broth. Bake 20 minutes longer.

MEXICAN CHICKEN

1 large fryer, cut in pieces	1 green pepper, minced
1 teaspoon salt	1 cup fresh mushrooms,
⅛ teaspoon pepper	sliced thin
½ teaspoon paprika	1 cup canned tomatoes
¼ teaspoon orégano	2 envelopes chicken
½ teaspoon garlic powder	bouillon, or 2 cubes
1 onion, minced	1 cup water

Mix salt, pepper, paprika, orégano, and garlic powder and rub into chicken pieces. Brown in heavy skillet. Add onions and peppers and brown, stirring frequently. Add all remaining ingredients. Cover. Cook 30 to 45 minutes or until chicken is tender and sauce is reduced.

OPEN-FACED CHICKEN SUPREME

4 slices chicken roll (from delicatessen)
1 slice white toast
¼ cucumber, sliced paper thin
Salt and pepper
1 green pepper ring

Cover toast slice with cucumber slices. Lay chicken roll on top. Sprinkle with salt and pepper and garnish with green pepper ring on top of all.

ORIENTAL CHICKEN

1 frying chicken, cut up
Salt and pepper
1 cup fresh pineapple juice
⅛ cup lemon juice
1½ cups water
1 teaspoon soy sauce
4 envelopes chicken bouillon powder, or equivalent
1½ cups fresh pineapple in chunks
2 stalks celery, cut up
1 can Chinese vegetables

Sprinkle chicken pieces with salt and pepper. Brown in heavy skillet. Remove. Add pineapple juice, lemon juice, water, and soy sauce. Bring to boil and dissolve chicken bouillon concentrate in this mixture. Replace chicken pieces. Simmer ½ hour. Add pineapple chunks, celery, and Chinese vegetables. Simmer 5 to 8 minutes longer.

CHICKEN LIVER KEBAB

1 pound chicken livers
1 green pepper cut in squares
1 can whole mushrooms (fresh may be used)
1 onion, cut in slices
Salt and pepper

On skewers, alternate chicken livers, green pepper, mushrooms, and onion slices. Season with salt and pepper. Broil, turning frequently.

CHICKEN LIVER BROIL

1 pound chicken livers
6 whole fresh mushrooms, sliced
1 green pepper, cut up
1 fresh tomato, cut up
1 small onion, grated
½ teaspoon garlic powder
Salt
Freshly ground black pepper

Arrange chicken livers and cut-up vegetables on sheet of foil in flat pan. Sprinkle with grated onion, garlic powder, salt, and pepper. Broil, turning frequently.

CHICKEN LIVERS ALOHA

1 pound chicken livers
½ teaspoon celery salt
½ teaspoon onion salt
½ teaspoon paprika
1 teaspoon curry powder
1 apple, diced
¼ medium pineapple, peeled and diced
¼ cup soy sauce
2 tablespoons water

Sprinkle livers with celery salt, onion salt, paprika, and curry powder. Toss lightly with apple and pineapple. Mix soy sauce and water. Pour over livers and fruit. Let stand at least 30 minutes. Cook over low heat about 30 minutes.

CHOPPED CHICKEN LIVERS

1 pound chicken livers
1 envelope onion bouillon powder, or equivalent
1 cup water
3 hard-boiled eggs
1 large raw onion
1 stalk celery
Salt and pepper

Put livers, onion bouillon concentrate and water in pan. Simmer slowly about 20 minutes or until livers are done. Put cooked, cooled livers, hard-boiled eggs, raw onion, and celery stalk through meat grinder. Season with salt and pepper.

CHOPPED CHICKEN LIVERS GOURMET

Prepare same as Chopped Chicken Livers recipe, but eliminate stalk of celery and add ¼ cup freshly squeezed orange juice instead.

TURKEY DIVAN

- **4 large slices leftover roast turkey**
- **1 package frozen broccoli spears**
- **1 slice American cheese**
- **½ teaspoon paprika**

Cook broccoli according to directions on package. In flat baking pan, lay out turkey slices. Place ¼ of the cooked broccoli spears on each slice. Lay ¼ slice cheese on top of each portion of broccoli. Sprinkle with paprika. Broil until cheese is browned and bubbly. (Meal number 2.)

THINK THIN

TURKEY CURRY HAWAIIAN

- **1 cup water**
- **1 envelope chicken bouillon powder, or equivalent**
- **½ cup minced onion**
- **3 teaspoons curry powder**
- **1 teaspoon salt**
- **½ teaspoon monosodium glutamate**
- **¼ teaspoon ginger**
- **2 cups diced leftover turkey**
- **1 cup cubed fresh pineapple**
- **1 can bean sprouts**

Mix water, chicken bouillon concentrate, onion, curry powder, salt, monosodium glutamate, and ginger in heavy skillet and bring to boil. Simmer slowly until liquid is half reduced. Add turkey and pineapple. Heat. Pour over bed of heated bean sprouts.

CHEESE

OPEN-FACED DANISH DELIGHT

1 slice white toast
1 slice Cheddar cheese
1 green pepper ring
1 thin slice tomato

Lay slice of cheese on slice of toast. Place pepper ring on top of cheese and fit tomato slice inside of pepper ring. Broil.

PIZZA

1 slice enriched white bread
2 thin slices Muenster cheese
1 tablespoon canned tomato sauce
⅛ teaspoon orégano
⅛ teaspoon garlic salt

Toast bread lightly. Place cheese slices on top. Place tomato sauce on top of cheese and sprinkle with orégano and garlic salt. Broil.

CHEESE SOUFFLÉ

- 1 slice white bread
- 1 slice American cheese
- 1 egg
- ½ cup skim milk
- Salt and pepper
- ½ teaspoon Worcestershire sauce
- ½ teaspoon paprika

Preheat oven to 375°. Place bread in bottom of individual casserole. Lay cheese slice on top of bread. Mix all other ingredients thoroughly and pour over bread and cheese. Bake 45 minutes until puffy and browned. (Meal number 2 only.)

"DANISH PASTRY"

- 1 slice white toast
- ¼ cup cottage cheese
- ½ envelope artificial sweetener, or equivalent
- Dash of nutmeg, dash of cinnamon

Spread cottage cheese on top of toast. Sprinkle with spices. Broil.

GLORIFIED MUSHROOMS

- 6 large fresh mushroom caps
- ½ cup cottage cheese
- 1 envelope onion bouillon powder, or 1 cube

Mix cottage cheese with onion bouillon concentrate. Stuff mushroom caps with this mixture. Broil until brown and bubbly on top.

EGGPLANT PARMESAN

1 medium eggplant
1 sliced fresh tomato
¼ pound sliced mozzarella cheese
½ teaspoon orégano

Preheat oven to 375°. Peel and slice eggplant and soak in water for 1 hour. Drain. Place slices in shallow baking dish. Place a slice of tomato and a slice of cheese on each eggplant slice. Sprinkle with orégano. Bake for 1 hour. (Meal number 2.)

HOT APPLE PIE WITH CHEESE

1 baked apple (See Index.)
1 slice white bread
¼ cup cottage cheese

Flatten baked apple on top of bread. Spread cottage cheese over apple. Pour juice of the baked apple over all. Broil until cheese bubbles.

SPRING GARDEN SALAD

1 whole green pepper
½ cup cottage cheese
1 pimiento, minced
1 stalk celery, minced
1 tablespoon onion, minced
Lettuce leaf
6 radish roses

Mix cottage cheese with pimiento, celery, and onion. Cut top off pepper and remove seeds. Stuff pepper with cottage cheese mixture. Serve upright on lettuce leaf, garnished with radish roses.

VEGETABLES

Note: All vegetable recipes marked *Unlimited* may be consumed in unlimited quantities at meals or at any time of the day or night for between-meal snacking.

BAKED ACORN SQUASH

　1 green acorn squash
　⅛ cup water
　⅛ teaspoon nutmeg
　¼ teaspoon cinnamon
　½ envelope artificial sweetener, or equivalent

Preheat oven to 375°. Pour water into shallow baking dish. Cut acorn squash in half lengthwise and scoop out seeds. Place squash skin side down in baking dish. Sprinkle with spices and sweetener. Bake for 1 hour.

BAKED ZUCCHINI SQUASH

　3 large zucchini squash
　1 can tomato purée
　1 tablespoon chopped parsley
　1 tablespoon basil
　¼ teaspoon garlic powder
　Salt and pepper
　¼ pound mozzarella cheese, sliced thin

Preheat oven to 350°. Simmer tomato purée and all seasonings in saucepan 30 minutes. Cut zucchini crosswise in ½-inch slices. Cover bottom of baking dish with sauce and add layer of zucchini. Then layer of cheese, layer of zucchini, etc. Top with remaining sauce and sprinkle with additional basil and parsley. Bake 1 hour. (Meal number 2 only.)

ZUCCHINI FIRENZE

4 medium zucchini squash
1 slice onion, cut up
1 envelope chicken bouillon powder, or 1 cube
⅛ cup water
¼ cup tomato juice
Salt and pepper

Combine all ingredients and simmer until tender or about
20 minutes. *Unlimited.*

ZUCCHINI NINA

1 pound can whole Italian-style tomatoes
2 large zucchini peeled and cut in rounds
2 green peppers cut in strips
1 onion cut in rounds
½ teaspoon basil
Salt and pepper

Combine all ingredients and simmer until tender or about
20 minutes.

CREAMED BROCCOLI

1 package frozen chopped broccoli
1 envelope chicken bouillon powder, or equivalent
¼ teaspoon nutmeg
¼ teaspoon garlic salt
¼ cup skim milk

Place all ingredients in blender. Blend until mixed. Heat.

BROCCOLI ESPAGNOLE

1 bunch broccoli	Pinch Cayenne pepper
Salted water	⅛ teaspoon black pepper
2 tablespoons onion, minced	1 envelope artificial sweetener, or equivalent
2 tablespoons green pepper, minced	1 teaspoon chili powder
1 1-pound can tomatoes	1 tablespoon grated Parmesan cheese
1 teaspoon salt	

Preheat oven to 350°. Cook broccoli in salted water until tender. Place in casserole and set aside. Combine all other ingredients except cheese and mix thoroughly. Pour over broccoli. Sprinkle with cheese. Cover. Bake ½ hour.

CAULIFLOWER SPECIAL

1 small head cauliflower
1 teaspoon garlic salt
1 teaspoon sauté onion (a prepared condiment)

Separate cauliflower buds and place in frying pan in enough water to cover buds. Sprinkle liberally with garlic salt and sauté onion. Cover and steam until tender. *Unlimited.*

"MASHED POTATOES"

1 head fresh cauliflower
Salted water
⅛ cup skim milk
Salt and pepper
⅛ teaspoon paprika

Cook cauliflower in salted water until tender. Break up in pieces with fork and place in blender. Add skim milk and salt and pepper. Whip thoroughly. Spoon out into small casserole. Sprinkle with paprika. Place in hot oven until bubbly. *Unlimited*.

CAULIFLOWER SUPREME

1 whole head cauliflower
⅛ teaspoon salt and pepper
⅛ teaspoon paprika
½ slice American cheese, grated

Preheat oven to 375°. Cook cauliflower in salted water until tender. Place whole head carefully in small casserole. Sprinkle with salt and pepper, paprika, and grated cheese. Bake for 15 minutes.

GOURMET CABBAGE

1 head cabbage, quartered
2 cups water
2 envelopes onion bouillon powder, or equivalent
½ teaspoon salt

Place all ingredients in deep saucepan. Simmer until tender. *Unlimited*.

SWEET AND SOUR RED CABBAGE

1 head red cabbage, shredded
1 medium can tomatoes
2 green peppers, chopped
1 onion, chopped
⅛ cup vinegar
3 tablespoons lemon juice
1 envelope artificial sweetener, or equivalent
Salt and pepper

Simmer all ingredients about 25 minutes.

SPINACH LOUISE

Fresh spinach
Salted water
2 tablespoons horseradish

Cook fresh spinach in salted water, Drain. Toss with horseradish. Serve. *Unlimited.*

VEGETABLE PIE

1 head cauliflower
Salted water
1 package frozen chopped spinach
⅛ cup dry skim milk powder
2 stalks celery, very finely diced
1 small green pepper, very finely diced
Salt and pepper

Cook cauliflower in salted water until tender. Remove from water and mash. Add spinach and skim milk. Whip thoroughly. Add celery, green pepper, salt, and pepper. Mound in casserole. Brown under broiler. *Unlimited.*

VEGETABLE PANCAKE

Mix leftover Vegetable Pie with:
1 slice white toast crumbed in blender
1 egg
1 slice cheese

Brown on both sides in heavy skillet. Melt 1 slice cheese on top during final few minutes of cooking. (Meal number 2 only.)

BEAN SPROUT SNACK

1 can bean sprouts, drained
⅛ teaspoon freshly ground black pepper
1 teaspoon garlic salt

Spread bean sprouts evenly in large pie plate. Sprinkle with garlic salt and pepper. Brown in oven until dry, stirring and turning frequently. *Unlimited*.

BEAN SPROUTS PARISIENNE

1 can bean sprouts, with liquid
2 scallions, diced
1 green pepper, diced
1 can mushroom pieces (with liquid)
1 stalk celery, diced
1 envelope chicken bouillon powder, or 1 cube

Combine all ingredients and simmer 20 minutes. *Unlimited*.

VEGETABLE CHOW MEIN

1 can bean sprouts with liquid
1 tablespoon shredded onion
1 can mushroom pieces
1 envelope onion bouillon powder, or cube
½ cup tomato juice
½ teaspoon garlic salt
Pepper

Combine all ingredients. Simmer 20 minutes.

GARLIC ARTICHOKE

1 artichoke	½ teaspoon salt
1 teaspoon garlic powder	1 cup water

Place all ingredients in deep saucepan. Simmer until artichoke can be easily pierced with fork.

MINTED CARROTS

4 carrots, peeled and cut in thin strips
1 teaspoon chopped fresh mint leaves
1 envelope artificial sweetener, or equivalent

Cook carrots in small amount boiling salted water until tender. Drain. Mix mint leaves and sweetener and toss with carrots.

GLORIFIED GREEN BEANS

1 can whole green beans
1 can tomatoes, drained
1 envelope chicken bouillon powder, or equivalent
1 teaspoon dried onion flakes
⅛ teaspoon basil

Preheat oven to 350°. Mix all ingredients well. Bake 20 minutes.

FRIED PEPPERS

2 frying peppers, cut in strips
¼ cup water
¼ envelope chicken bouillon powder, or 1 cube
½ teaspoon salt

Brown strips of pepper in heavy skillet. When skin blisters, add remaining ingredients. Cook until liquid is absorbed.

MIXED VEGETABLES

    1 envelope onion bouillon powder, or 1 cube
    1 envelope vegetable bouillon powder, or 1 cube
    1 small can cooked okra
    1½ cups water
    ½ green pepper, sliced
    3 slices onion
    1 stalk celery, chopped (with leaves)

Place all ingredients in saucepan and simmer 15 minutes. Drain broth and drink as vegetable consommé. Serve drained vegetables separately.

MUSHROOM NASCH

    1 pound fresh mushrooms
    Water to cover
    Salt and pepper
    Onion powder
    Garlic powder

Wash and stem mushrooms and cut into small pieces. Place in saucepan with water just to cover. Add seasoning to taste. Cook slowly until tender. Drain. Keep refrigerated for between-meal nibbling. (Also excellent for garnish, extra vegetable, or in bouillon.) *Unlimited*.

MUSHROOMS SAUTÉ

    1 pound fresh mushrooms
    ½ teaspoon rosemary
    ½ teaspoon orégano
    1 envelope chicken bouillon powder, or 1 cube
    ½ cup water
    ¼ teaspoon Worcestershire sauce
    Salt and pepper

Place all ingredients except mushrooms in large heavy frying pan. Place washed whole mushrooms cap side down in this mixture. Simmer very slowly, basting frequently, until liquid is absorbed. *Unlimited.*

SPICY PICKLED BEETS

1 can sliced beets with juices
1 small onion, sliced
¼ cup vinegar
½ envelope artificial sweetener, or equivalent

Combine all ingredients in bowl. Refrigerate at least 2 hours before serving to blend flavors.

TURNIP WHIP

1 whole turnip (yellow)
Water to cover
Salt
Pepper (optional)
1 envelope onion bouillon powder, or 1 cube

Peel turnip and cut in pieces. Place in a saucepan with water to cover. Add salt and onion bouillon concentrate. Cook slowly until tender. (About 25-30 minutes.) Drain. Mash with potato masher. Then whip thoroughly with fork. Sprinkle with salt and pepper if desired.

BRAISED CELERY

1 bunch celery
Water to cover
Salt
1 envelope chicken bouillon powder, or equivalent

Wash celery and cut in 1″ pieces. Place in saucepan with water to cover. Add salt and chicken bouillon concentrate. Bring to boil and cook until celery is tender. Drain and serve. *Unlimited*.

STUFFED WHOLE CABBAGE

1 small head cabbage
1 minced onion
1 clove garlic, minced
¼ cup minced green pepper
¼ cup finely diced celery
½ cup tomato juice
1 teaspoon Worcestershire sauce
Salt and pepper

Preheat oven to 325°. Wash cabbage. Cut out core, plus an extra half inch. Cook head in boiling salted water, covered, for 20 minutes. Drain. Sauté onion, garlic, green pepper, and celery in small amount water for 10 minutes. Add tomato juice, Worcestershire sauce, salt, and pepper. Blend mixture well. Pour into cabbage spaces. Bake, covered, stuffed side up for 1 hour. Cut into wedges to serve.

SAUCED ASPARAGUS

1 pound fresh asparagus
Soy sauce or Worcestershire sauce

Brown whole asparagus in tiny amount water in heavy skillet, turning constantly. Add enough soy or Worcestershire sauce to coat asparagus. Bring to boiling point, turning spears to coat thoroughly with sauce. Serve hot or cold. *Unlimited*.

ESCAROLE ITALIENNE

1 head escarole, washed and cut up
½ cup water
1 package chicken bouillon powder, or 1 cube
Salt to taste

Cook all ingredients together until escarole is tender. *Unlimited.*

CARROT ZUCCHINI BAKE

4 carrots, peeled and sliced thin
4 zucchini, sliced thin
2 tablespoons minced fresh onion
½ cup chicken bouillon
2 tablespoons lemon juice
Salt and pepper

Preheat oven to 350°. Combine all ingredients in baking dish. Bake for 1 hour.

ROASTED PEPPERS

Preheat oven to 350°. Put whole peppers in pan in bottom of oven. Turn every 10 minutes until skin is brown. Let cool and peel skin. Season with salt or garlic powder. *Unlimited.*

ITALIAN GREEN BEANS

1 package frozen Italian beans, cooked
1 tomato, diced
½ cup diced green pepper
1 tablespoon minced onion
⅛ teaspoon rosemary
⅛ teaspoon basil
Salt and pepper

Combine tomato, green pepper, onion, rosemary, and basil in saucepan with ¼ cup bean liquid. Cook slowly until pepper is tender. Add cooked green beans and salt and pepper. Heat through and serve.

McINTOSH CABBAGE

1 small onion, diced
1 envelope bouillon, or equivalent
Juice of ¼ lemon
1 envelope sweetener, or equivalent
1 McIntosh apple (with skin) diced
1 head cabbage, shredded

Brown diced onion in bouillon with tiny amount water. Add remaining ingredients. Cook slowly, adding water very sparingly if needed. It will be light brown by the time cabbage is cooked.

"POTATO" PUDDING

1 head cauliflower
2 tablespoons dried minced onion
1 bouillon cube, or 1 envelope
½ teaspoon seasoned salt
½ teaspoon grated cheese

Preheat oven to 350°. Cook cauliflower in water and bouillon cube until very soft. Mash with potato masher. Add minced dried onion and mix well. Season to taste with salt and pepper. Place in casserole and spread flat. Sprinkle top with seasoned salt and grated cheese. Bake until dark golden brown on top. *Unlimited.*

EGGPLANT AND MUSHROOMS

1 onion, minced
½ pound mushrooms, sliced
1 eggplant, peeled and cubed
½ cup beef bouillon
½ clove garlic, crushed
Salt and pepper to taste

Cook all ingredients in covered saucepan slowly for about 1 hour.

EGGPLANT ITALIAN

1 eggplant, peeled and cubed
1 green pepper, diced
1 onion, diced
1 clove garlic, minced
Salt and pepper
¼ teaspoon orégano
1 cup tomato juice

Cook all ingredients slowly in covered saucepan for about 1 hour.

STRING BEANS GOURMET

1 package frozen French-style string beans
1 bay leaf
1 cup beef bouillon

Simmer all ingredients together for about 10 minutes. *Unlimited.*

SALADS

Note: Salad recipes marked *Unlimited* may be consumed in unlimited quantities at meals or between meals.

ZIPPY COLE SLAW

1 medium head cabbage, shredded
3 carrots, grated
2 green peppers, diced
1 small onion, grated

Mix all vegetables together.

Zippy Cole Slaw Dressing:

¼ cup white vinegar
½ cup water
1 teaspoon prepared mustard
2 drops liquid artificial sweetener, or equivalent
Salt and pepper

Mix all dressing ingredients in blender or beat with egg beater.

Pour dressing over mixed vegetables and let stand at least 1 hour to blend flavors. *Unlimited.*

SWEET AND SOUR CUCUMBER SALAD

1 large cucumber, peeled and sliced
⅓ cup white vinegar
1 envelope artificial sweetener or equivalent
1 tablespoon finely minced fresh parsley

Mix all ingredients. Chill. *Unlimited.*

JELLIED CABBAGE SALAD

1 envelope unflavored gelatin
½ envelope artificial sweetener, or equivalent
½ teaspoon salt
1½ cups water
¼ cup lemon juice
1½ cups finely shredded cabbage
¼ cup sliced radishes
¼ cup finely cut scallions

Mix gelatin, sweetener, salt, and ½ cup water in saucepan. Place over low heat, stirring constantly until gelatin is completely dissolved. Remove from heat and stir in remaining 1 cup water and lemon juice. Chill mixture to unbeaten egg white consistency. Fold in cabbage, radishes, and scallions. Turn into mold and chill until firm. *Unlimited.*

TOMATO ASPIC

3 cups tomato juice
1 stalk celery, cut in large pieces
2 lemon slices
1 bay leaf
1 small onion, sliced
¼ cup vinegar
1 teaspoon salt
¼ teaspoon black pepper
2 envelopes gelatin
⅔ cup additional tomato juice, kept cold
1½ cup chopped minced raw vegetables (your preference)

Combine 3 cups tomato juice, celery, lemon, bay leaf, onion, vinegar, salt, and pepper. Simmer uncovered for 10 minutes. Strain. Sprinkle gelatin over the ⅔ cup cold tomato juice to soften; stir in hot strained tomato mixture

225

until well dissolved. Chill to consistency of unbeaten egg white, stirring occasionally. Fold in raw vegetables. Spoon into mold. Chill until firm.

PERFECTION SALAD

1 envelope unflavored gelatin
¼ cup water
1 cup boiling water
½ envelope artificial sweetener, or equivalent
⅓ cup vinegar

Juice of 2 lemons
½ cup chopped celery
½ cup shredded cabbage
½ cup chopped green pepper
Small jar pimientos, drained and cut fine

Dissolve gelatin in ¼ cup cold water. Stir in boiling water. Then add all other ingredients. Mix well. Chill until firm. *Unlimited*.

STOP AND GO SALAD

1 bunch fresh watercress
½ cup sliced radishes
Juice of 1 lemon

Freshly ground black pepper
Salt

Toss all ingredients lightly. *Unlimited*.

HEARTS OF ARTICHOKE SALAD

½ cup canned, drained artichoke hearts
1 pimiento, cut in thin strips
4 radishes, thinly sliced
3 thin slices onion

⅛ cup wine vinegar
¼ teaspoon garlic salt
Black pepper, freshly ground
Lettuce leaves

Combine all ingredients except lettuce leaves. Toss lightly. Serve mixture on lettuce leaves.

STUFFED PEPPER SALAD

1 large green pepper	1 tablespoon minced
¼ cup diced cucumber	chives
¼ cup diced raw kohlrabi	⅛ cup wine vinegar
¼ cup diced celery	Salt and pepper
⅛ cup diced radishes	

Cut top from pepper and remove seeds. Mix all other ingredients. Stuff this mixture into pepper. Serve on bed of lettuce. *Unlimited*.

SALAD DELIGHT

1 cucumber, diced
1 wedge cabbage, shredded fine
1 scallion, diced fine
⅛ cup wine vinegar
2 drops liquid artificial sweetener, or equivalent
Salt and pepper

Mix wine vinegar, sweetener, salt, and pepper and pour over mixed raw vegetables. Serve on lettuce leaf and garnish with radish roses. *Unlimited*.

CABBAGE SUISSE

½ head cabbage	2 envelopes onion bouil-
1 slice onion, cut in strips	lon powder, or equiva-
1 cucumber, cut in thin	lent
strips	2 envelopes artificial
1 green pepper, cut in	sweetener, or equiva-
thin strips	lent
	¼ cup wine vinegar

Shred cabbage and place in deep bowl with other vegetables. Mix onion bouillon concentrate, sweetener, and wine

227

vinegar. Pour over vegetables and mix well. Allow to stand 3 to 4 hours without refrigerating. *Unlimited*.

ANTIPASTO THINK THIN

¼ head cauliflower, broken into small buds
1 jar pimientos, cut in strips
1 green pepper, cut in rings
1 teaspoon garlic salt
⅛ cup wine vinegar

Arrange vegetables attractively on small plate. Mix wine vinegar and garlic salt, and pour over vegetables. *Unlimited*.

VARIETY SALAD

4 tablespoons vinegar
2 tablespoons cold water
1 clove garlic, crushed
¼ teaspoon salt
⅛ teaspoon paprika
¼ teaspoon artificial powdered sweetener
1 tablespoon chopped chives
¼ head cauliflower, thinly sliced
1 cucumber, thinly sliced
1 small carrot, grated fine

Mix vinegar, water, garlic, salt, paprika, sweetener, and chives thoroughly. Pour over vegetables. Mix well. Chill. *Unlimited*.

BEET SALAD

½ cup chopped canned beets
1½ cups chopped raw cabbage
1 tablespoon horseradish
3 tablespoons vinegar
2 drops liquid artificial sweetener
Salt and pepper

Combine all ingredients and mix well. Chill.

ORIENTAL SALAD

1 can bean sprouts,
drained
1 scallion, finely chopped
¼ cup thinly sliced
pimiento
2 tablespoons ground se-
same seeds

2 tablespoons soy sauce
2 tablespoons vinegar
1 clove garlic, finely
chopped
Salt and pepper

Combine all ingredients except bean sprouts. Mix well.
Pour over bean sprouts and toss gently. Chill at least 1 hour
before serving. *Unlimited.*

SALAD CEYLON

1 Bermuda onion, finely sliced
1 cucumber, finely sliced
1 green pepper, finely sliced
Juice of 1 lemon
Freshly ground black pepper
Salt

Combine all ingredients and mix well. Chill.

NEAPOLITAN SALAD

1 clove garlic
1 head fennel, thinly sliced
1 head chicory, torn into bite-size pieces
1 large fresh tomato, cut in bite-size wedges
3 tablespoons wine vinegar
Salt and freshly ground pepper

Toss all ingredients together. Serve at once.

SUNSHINE SALAD

½ cup cooked pineapple, well drained
2 raw carrots, grated
1 recipe Think Thin orange gelatin (See Index.)

Crush pineapple in blender. Fold crushed pineapple and grated carrots into orange gelatin mixture and chill to set. Serve on lettuce as salad. Equals ½ a fruit and your ½ cup limited vegetable for the day.

STRINGBEAN SALAD

Cold French-style string beans
Salt and pepper
Dash garlic powder
1 scallion, minced
Sprinkle of vinegar

Mix all ingredients and refrigerate. *Unlimited*.

RED AND GREEN SALAD

2 sweet red peppers, thin sliced
2 green peppers, thin sliced
1 large onion, thin sliced
2 tablespoons vinegar
2 tablespoons water
1 teaspoon salt
2 envelopes artificial sweetener, or equivalent

Mix all ingredients and stir well. Chill several hours or overnight. *Unlimited*.

BEAN SPROUT SALAD

1 can bean sprouts,
drained
1 can French-style string
beans
1 can French-style wax
beans
½ cup chopped onion

¼ cup vinegar
1½ envelopes artificial
sweetener, or equiva-
lent
1 tablespoon soy sauce
1 teaspoon dry mustard
Salt and pepper

Combine all ingredients and mix well. Refrigerate 3 to 4 hours before serving.

PICKLED BEAN SALAD

1 can French-style string beans
1 can French-style wax beans
1 green pepper, diced
1 small onion, chopped
⅓ cup vinegar
Artificial sweetener to taste

Mix all ingredients. Let stand at least 2 hours to mingle flavors.

BROCCOLI SALAD

Raw broccoli flowerets,
cut up
1 small tomato,
cut in wedges
Few onion rings
Chicory

Lettuce
⅛ cup wine vinegar
¼ teaspoon garlic powder
¼ teaspoon Italian
seasoning
Salt and pepper

Toss broccoli, tomato, onion, chicory, and lettuce in a wooden bowl. Mix vinegar, garlic powder, Italian seasoning, salt, and pepper and pour over vegetables.

FRESH MUSHROOM SALAD

1 cup water
1 tablespoon lemon juice
½ pound fresh mushrooms, sliced
¼ cup skim milk
1 tablespoon instant minced onion flakes
Artificial sweetener to equal 1 teaspoon sugar
½ teaspoon salt
⅛ teaspoon white pepper

In saucepan, combine water and lemon juice. Bring to boil. Add mushrooms. Cover. Reduce heat. Simmer 3 minutes. Drain mushrooms and pat dry. Combine all other ingredients in bowl. Add mushrooms and toss lightly. Serve on raw spinach leaves. Can be served hot or cold and may be used as snack. *Unlimited.*

SAUCES AND DRESSINGS

SAUCES FOR MEATS AND FISH

MARINARA SAUCE

1 1-pound can whole Italian-style tomatoes
1 clove garlic, crushed
¼ teaspoon basil
⅛ teaspoon cinnamon
Salt and pepper

Put tomatoes in blender to purée. Place in saucepan. When tomato purée comes to a simmer, add garlic, basil, cinnamon, salt, and pepper. Cover. Cook slowly for 1 hour, stirring often.

TARTAR SAUCE (good with fish)

¼ cup cottage cheese
2 tablespoons minced sour pickle
1 tablespoon minced onion
Salt and pepper

Mix thoroughly and whip with fork. Use sparingly.

COCKTAIL SAUCE (for seafood)

½ cup tomato juice
1 teaspoon horseradish
½ teaspoon parsley flakes
½ teaspoon lemon juice
Dash Tabasco
Salt and pepper

Blend all ingredients. Chill and serve.

COCKTAIL SAUCE LOUISIANA

4 ounces boiled-down tomato juice (simmer
   until reduced to half its original quantity)
1 tablespoon horseradish
½ teaspoon Worcestershire sauce
⅛ teaspoon chili powder
1-2 drops Louisiana Hot Sauce
1 teaspoon lemon juice
½ teaspoon salt
4 drops liquid artificial sweetener

Mix all ingredients well and chill.

BASTING SAUCE

1 envelope onion bouillon powder, or 1 cube
1 teaspoon chopped onion
½ cup water
1 clove garlic, minced
¼ cup chopped green pepper
¼ cup chopped celery
½ cup tomato juice (optional)
Salt and pepper

Simmer all ingredients until vegetables are tender. Use to baste fish or meat. If thinner sauce is desired, add a little more water.

CRANBERRY RELISH (good with poultry)

1 cup washed fresh cranberries
1 unpeeled orange with seeds removed
1 envelope artificial sweetener, or equivalent

Put cranberries and cut-up orange through grinder. Add sweetener. Mix well. Chill to blend flavors. (½-cup serving equals 1 fruit.)

RELISH

12 large tomatoes
2 large onions
1½ large green or red peppers
3 large stalks celery
1 clove garlic, finely minced
¼ teaspoon dry mustard
¼ cup cider vinegar
4 envelopes artificial sweetener, or equivalent
2 teaspoons salt
⅛ teaspoon freshly ground black pepper
2 teaspoons allspice

Scald tomatoes and peel. Cut up in large kettle. Grind onions, peppers, and celery. Add to tomatoes. Add remaining ingredients. Bring to boil. Simmer 2½ to 3 hours until quite thick. May be canned or frozen. Serve with meats.

STUFFINGS FOR MEAT, FISH, AND POULTRY

THINK THIN STUFFING

Day old bread, cubed	1 teaspoon poultry
Chopped celery	seasoning
Chopped onion	Little warm water
Salt and pepper	

Amounts of bread, onion, and celery will depend on size of bird to be stuffed. Combine all ingredients and use to stuff turkey, chicken, Cornish game hen, etc. (½ cup allowed if bread for Meal number 2 is eliminated.)

VEGETABLE STUFFING FOR POULTRY

Grated raw carrot	Poultry seasoning
Grated onion	Salt and pepper to taste
Grated celery	

Amounts will depend on size of poultry to be stuffed. Mix all ingredients and stuff cavity.

MUSHROOM STUFFING

1 envelope onion bouillon powder, or 1 cube
¼ cup water
¾ cup chopped mushrooms
1 tablespoon grated onion
½ teaspoon poultry seasoning
½ teaspoon salt
Dash cayenne

Mix onion bouillon concentrate with water in small frying pan. Sauté mushrooms and onions in this mixture until tender. Mix in seasonings. Use as stuffing for poultry, meat, or fish. *Unlimited.*

SALAD DRESSINGS

GARLIC VINEGAR

1 cup vinegar   4 cloves garlic

Heat vinegar to boiling point. Add garlic. Put in covered container. When cool, store in refrigerator.

PIMIENTO FRENCH DRESSING

½ teaspoon dry mustard
½ teaspoon paprika
½ teaspoon salt
¼ teaspoon pepper
2 tablespoons lemon juice
2 tablespoons wine vinegar

⅔ cup chicken bouillon
1 clove garlic
3 tablespoons sliced pimientos
1 envelope artificial sweetener, or equivalent

Combine all ingredients in blender and blend thoroughly. Store covered in refrigerator.

TARRAGON DRESSING

½ small bottle wine vinegar
Salt and pepper to taste
3 cloves garlic
½ teaspoon basil
½ teaspoon tarragon
1 teaspoon minced raw onion
3 tablespoons tomato juice

Blend in blender. Store covered in refrigerator.

SALAD DRESSING NAPOLITANO

1 small can tomato juice
¼ cup wine vinegar
Artificial sweetener to taste
Salt and pepper to taste
Few dashes Worcester-
  shire sauce
¼ teaspoon horseradish

¼ teaspoon garlic powder
¼ teaspoon orégano
¼ teaspoon onion powder
  or flakes
¼ teaspoon basil leaves
¼ teaspoon powdered
  thyme

Blend all ingredients at high speed for a few minutes. Let stand in uncovered jar for 1 hour. Cover and refrigerate.

CUCUMBER DRESSING

1 cup tomato juice
¼ cup vinegar
1 teaspoon minced onion
2 tablespoons minced cucumber
½ teaspoon lemon juice
Salt and pepper

Shake ingredients well in tightly covered jar. Store in refrigerator.

"FRENCH" DRESSING FOR SALADS

½ cup tomato juice
2 tablespoons lemon juice
¼ teaspoon dry mustard
¼ teaspoon paprika
1 teaspoon minced onion
⅛ teaspoon freshly ground black pepper
⅛ teaspoon salt
¼ teaspoon horseradish

Shake well in glass jar. Keep under refrigeration.

"SOUR CREAM" SALAD DRESSING

  2 tablespoons cottage cheese
  1 teaspoon lemon juice
  2 teaspoons skim milk
  ⅛ teaspoon salt

Whip all ingredients together until smooth. (Use sparingly.)

SALAD DRESSING PIQUANT

  ¼ cup vinegar
  1 envelope chicken bouillon powder
  ¼ teaspoon garlic salt
  2 drops liquid artificial sweetener, or equivalent

Mix thoroughly and serve.

MANHATTAN SALAD DRESSING

  1 can mixed vegetable juices
  1 clove garlic
  ½ teaspoon prepared mustard
  ½ teaspoon Worcestershire sauce
  ⅛ teaspoon paprika

Shake well in glass jar. Store in refrigerator.

DRESSING ITALIANO

  ¼ cup cottage cheese
  2 tablespoons skim milk
  ¼ teaspoon orégano
  ⅛ teaspoon garlic powder
  ¼ teaspoon salt
  1 teaspoon grated Parmesan cheese

Whip all ingredients thoroughly. (Use sparingly.)

DESSERT SAUCES

LO-WHIP (dessert topping)

¼ cup cold water
1 tablespoon lemon juice
1 envelope artificial sweetener, or equivalent
3 tablespoons dry powdered skim milk

Combine all ingredients and chill in bowl. Chill egg beater. Just before serving, beat until mixture is stiff enough to stand in peaks. Use immediately. (Yields about 1 cup.)

MOCK STRAWBERRY JAM

¼ cup lemon flavor low-calorie soda
6 whole strawberries (fresh or frozen)
1 envelope artificial sweetener, or equivalent

Mash strawberries into soda in saucepan. Add sweetener. Boil 3 minutes. Let cool and refrigerate. (Equals 1 fruit.)

DESSERTS

ORANGE CHIFFON

1 can or bottle low-calorie orange soda
1 envelope unflavored gelatin

Dissolve gelatin in ¼ cup of the soda. Boil remaining soda. Add to gelatin-soda mixture. Stir thoroughly and refrigerate until set. Spoon into blender. Blend 3-4 minutes at high speed until mixture is pale and foamy. Pour into bowl. Refrigerate. *Unlimited.*

RASPBERRY CHIFFON

1 can or bottle low-calorie raspberry soda
1 envelope unflavored gelatin
6 whole strawberries (fresh or frozen)

Dissolve gelatin in ¼ cup of the soda. Boil remaining soda. Add to gelatin-soda mixture. Stir thoroughly and refrigerate until set. Spoon out into blender. Blend 3-4 minutes at high speed until mixture is pale and foamy. While mixture is blending, slice strawberries thin. Pour chiffon mixture into bowl and fold in strawberry slices. (Equals 1 fruit.)

BLACK CHERRY CHIFFON

1 can or bottle low-calorie black cherry soda
1 envelope unflavored gelatin
½ grapefruit, sectioned

Dissolve gelatin in ¼ cup soda. Boil remaining soda. Add to gelatin-soda mixture. Stir thoroughly and refrigerate until set. Spoon out into blender. Blend 3-4 minutes at high speed until mixture is pale and foamy. Pour into bowl and fold in grapefruit sections. (Equals 1 fruit.)

TROPICAL GELATIN

1 can or bottle low-calorie lemon soda
1 envelope unflavored gelatin
½ orange, sections cut up
¼ grapefruit, sections cut up

Dissolve gelatin in ¼ cup soda. Boil remaining soda and add to soda-gelatin mixture. Stir thoroughly and chill. When partially set, fold in fruit. Chill until set hard. (Equals 1 fruit.)

CUSTARD TREAT

2 cups skim milk
1 envelope unflavored gelatin
2 to 3 envelopes artificial sweetener, or equivalent
¼ teaspoon salt
1 teaspoon vanilla extract
4 drops yellow food coloring
½ teaspoon nutmeg

Stir gelatin into ½ cup of the milk to soften. Place over heat to dissolve, stirring constantly. Do not boil. Remove from heat. Add sweetener, salt, vanilla, 1½ cups remaining milk, and food coloring. Stir well. Pour into custard cups. Sprinkle with nutmeg. Chill until firm. (Equals milk allowance for one day.)

STRAWBERRY FLUFF

For each cup of Custard Treat (see Recipe) add 1 whole strawberry. Whip in blender. Will reset in few minutes.

PEACH FLUFF

For each cup of Custard Treat (see Recipe) add 1 generous slice of peeled fresh peach. Whip in blender. Will reset in few minutes.

PINEAPPLE FLUFF

For each cup of Custard Treat (see Recipe) add 2 or 3 cubes Pineapple Ambrosia (see Recipe). Whip in blender. Will reset in few minutes.

JEWEL PARFAIT

1 can or bottle low-calorie black cherry or raspberry soda
1 can or bottle low-calorie lemon-lime soda
2 envelopes unflavored gelatin
1 tablespoon lemon juice
6 large strawberries, cut up
Few drops green food coloring

Soften 1 envelope gelatin in ¼ cup of the black cherry or raspberry soda. Boil remaining cherry or raspberry soda. Add to soda-gelatin mixture.

Repeat same procedure with lemon-lime soda, also adding lemon juice and green food coloring.

Chill both mixtures until the consistency of unbeaten egg whites. In parfait glass, spoon in layer of red gelatin mixture, layer of cut-up strawberries, layer of green gelatin mixture. Repeat. Fills 3 to 4 parfait glasses. (Entire recipe equals 1 fruit.)

PUMPKIN CHIFFON PIE

1½ cups fresh or canned pumpkin
3 eggs, separated
¾ cup skimmed evaporated milk
2 teaspoons pumpkin pie spice
2 envelopes artificial sweetener, or equivalent
1 envelope gelatin dissolved in
2 tablespoons cold water
1 teaspoon orange extract
1 teaspoon lemon extract

In heavy saucepan, place pumpkin, slightly beaten egg yolks, milk, spice, and 1 envelope of the artificial sweetener. Cook, stirring constantly, until mixture thickens slightly.

Remove from heat and blend in gelatin which has been dissolved in water. Cool to room temperature. Add flavorings. Beat egg whites until thick, adding remaining artificial sweetener slowly. When peaks form, fold into pumpkin mixture. Spoon into 8″ pie plate. Chill. (To be served only on special occasions, such as holidays, because extra eggs are involved.)

STRAWBERRIES JUBILEE

   ¼ cup low-calorie lemon soda
   6 large whole strawberries
   ½ envelope artificial sweetener, or equivalent

Combine all ingredients and boil for 3 minutes. Cool and chill. (Equals 1 fruit.)

CARVEL

   1 envelope unflavored gelatin
   ½ cup boiling water
   ⅓ cup dry skim milk powder
   1 teaspoon instant coffee powder
   1 capful vanilla extract
   1 envelope artificial sweetener, or equivalent
   6 crushed ice cubes

Put gelatin in blender. Add boiling water. Beat. Add all other ingredients except ice. Beat until well mixed and dissolved. Gradually add crushed ice. Let stand 5 minutes.

CHERRY SURPRISE

   2 ounces low-calorie cherry soda
   ⅓ cup dry skim milk powder
   1 envelope artificial sweetener, or equivalent
   6 sliced strawberries

Mix soda, skim milk powder, and artificial sweetener in blender at high speed. Add strawberries and beat 2 minutes longer. Freeze for one hour. (Equals 1 fruit.)

TANGY ORANGE MOLD

1 envelope gelatin (un-
flavored)
½ cup water
1 tablespoon grated
orange rind
½ cup fresh orange juice

1 cup skim milk
1 envelope artificial
sweetener, or equiva-
lent
½ teaspoon vanilla extract
1 orange, sectioned

Soften gelatin in water and dissolve over low heat. Mix orange rind, orange juice, skim milk, artificial sweetener, and vanilla. Add dissolved gelatin mixture. Pour into mold and chill until set. Decorate with orange sections. (Equals 1 fruit.)

RAINBOW DESSERT

1 can or bottle low-
calorie strawberry soda
1 can or bottle low-
calorie lemon soda
1 can or bottle low-
calorie orange soda

3 envelopes unflavored
gelatin
3 strawberries, sliced
½ large apple, diced
½ orange, cut up

Dissolve 1 envelope gelatin in ¼ cup of the strawberry soda. Boil remaining strawberry soda and add to soda-gelatin mixture. Stir well and chill until the consistency of unbeaten egg white. Fold in sliced strawberries.

Repeat above procedure with lemon soda, folding in diced apple when chilled to consistency of unbeaten egg white.

Repeat above procedure with orange soda, folding in cut-up orange.

Spoon strawberry mixture into bottom of mold. Spoon lemon mixture on top of strawberry mixture. Spoon orange mixture on top of lemon mixture. Chill until firm. (Equals 1½ fruits.)

ORANGE SHERBET

1 cup skim milk
3 tablespoons frozen orange juice concentrate
½ envelope artificial sweetener, or equivalent

Mix all ingredients in blender. Pour into ice cube tray. Freeze. When almost solid, turn out of tray and beat with fork. Return to tray. Refreeze.

PINEAPPLE SHERBERT

1 cup skim milk
3 tablespoons frozen pineapple juice concentrate
½ envelope artificial sweetener, or equivalent

Mix all ingredients in blender. Pour into ice cube tray. Freeze. When almost solid, turn out of tray and beat with fork. Return to tray. Refreeze.

STRAWBERRY SHERBET

1 cup skim milk
3 large whole strawberries
½ envelope artificial sweetener, or equivalent

Mix all ingredients in blender. Pour into ice cube tray. Freeze. When almost solid, turn out of tray and beat with fork. Refreeze.

FRESH LEMON GELATIN

1 teaspoon unflavored gelatin
2 tablespoons cold water
½ cup water
1 tablespoon lemon juice
1 envelope artificial sweetener, or equivalent

Dissolve gelatin in 2 tablespoons cold water. Boil ½ cup water and add to gelatin mixture. Add remaining ingredients. Chill until set.

COFFEE GEL

1 teaspoon unflavored gelatin
1 envelope artificial sweetener, or equivalent
2 tablespoons cold water
½ cup very hot coffee

Dissolve gelatin in water. Add sweetener and coffee. Chill until set.

Note: For balanced nutrition and consequent retention of skin tone while eating to lose weight, 1 pint of skim milk must be consumed each day. Milk used in dessert recipes should be considered part of the daily milk requirement.

JELLO JEMS

1 can or bottle low-calorie orange soda
1 envelope unflavored gelatin

Dissolve gelatin in ¼ cup of the orange soda. Boil remaining soda and add to soda-gelatin mixture. Pour into ice cube tray. Refrigerate until set firm.

Repeat above procedure with black cherry gelatin.
Repeat above procedure with grape gelatin.

When all three trays are set firm, cut into squares. Mix in large bowl, alternating colors and flavors. *Unlimited.*

STRAWBERRY ICE CREAM

6 whole strawberries, fresh or frozen
½ cup skim milk powder
¼ cup low-calorie wild strawberry soda

Blend berries and soda in blender. Add skim milk powder very slowly. Pour into ice cube tray and freeze. (Equals 1 fruit.)

PUMPKIN CUSTARD

4 ounces pumpkin (canned or fresh)
½ cup evaporated skim milk
2 envelopes artificial sweetener
1 teaspoon vanilla
¼ teaspoon cinnamon
½ teaspoon pumpkin pie spice

Preheat oven to 350°. Combine all ingredients and whip. Place in baking dish. Bake 1 hour or until silver knife inserted in center comes out clean. Equals ½ cup limited vegetable and ½ of your daily milk allowance.

FRUITS

Note: Men may have 5 different pieces of fruit each day. Women may have 3 different pieces of fruit each day. Fruit, however, is not obligatory. It is an option. Avoid the following fruits:

Bananas	Watermelon
Grapes	Avocado
Cherries	Dried fruits

FRUIT EQUIVALENTS

¼ fresh pineapple equals 1 fruit

½ canteloupe equals 1 fruit

2" wedge Honeydew, Cassava, Persian melon equals 1 fruit

½ cup blueberries equals 1 fruit

6 whole large strawberries equal 1 fruit

½ grapefruit equals 1 fruit

½ cup raspberries equals 1 fruit

1 cup rhubarb equals 1 fruit

PINEAPPLE AMBROSIA

1 whole fresh pineapple, peeled and cut in 1" pieces
1 can or bottle low-calorie orange soda
½ teaspoon cinnamon
½ teaspoon nutmeg
½ envelope artificial sweetener, or equivalent

Preheat oven to 350°. Place pineapple pieces in casserole. Pour orange soda over them. Sprinkle with spices and sweetener. Bake for about 1 hour. (One-fourth of a whole fresh pineapple equals 1 fruit. Therefore, one-fourth of entire casserole equals 1 fruit.)

BAKED APPLES

4 large baking apples (Rome Beauty, Cortland, etc.)
1 can low-calorie black cherry soda
½ teaspoon cinnamon
1 envelope artificial sweetener

Preheat oven to 375°. Wash and core apples and place in baking dish. Pour black cherry soda over them. Sprinkle with cinnamon and artificial sweetener. Bake for 1 hour.

ROSY BAKED PEARS

4 fresh pears
½ can or bottle low-calorie orange soda
½ teaspoon cinnamon

Preheat oven to 350°. Pour orange soda in baking dish and sprinkle with cinnamon. Stem pears and cut in half lengthwise. Arrange pears cut side down. Bake until soda has cooked away almost completely. Baste pears occasionally.

STEWED FRUIT

¼ fresh pineapple
1 pear
1 apple
1 can low-calorie black cherry soda
½ envelope artificial sweetener
¼ teaspoon nutmeg
¼ teaspoon cinnamon

Cut fruit into bite-sized pieces. Place in saucepan with black cherry soda and spices and sweetener. Simmer slowly for 1 hour. (⅓ of entire dish equals 1 fruit.)

FRESH FRUIT COMPOTE

  ½ grapefruit
  1 orange
  6 strawberries
  1 fresh peach

Section orange and grapefruit. Slice peach and straw-berries. Mix together in bowl. Refrigerate. (¼ bowl equals 1 fruit.)

BLUE-AND-GOLD SURPRISE

  ½ canteloupe
  ¼ cup blueberries
  1 portion Orange Chiffon (See recipe under Desserts.)

Scoop seeds out of canteloupe. Fill cavity with Orange Chiffon. Sprinkle blueberries on top. (Equals 1½ fruits, because ½ cup of blueberries would equal 1 fruit.)

APPLE PIE

  3 large apples
  ½ teaspoon cinnamon
  1 envelope artificial sweetener, or equivalent
  1 envelope unsweetened gelatin
  1 can Fresca
  ¼ cup dry skim milk powder

Preheat oven to 350°. Core apples, leaving skin on. Slice into pie plate. Sprinkle with cinnamon and artificial sweetener. Dissolve gelatin in ¼ cup of the Fresca. Boil remaining Fresca. Add to Fresca-gelatin mixture. Cool. Pour over apples. Sprinkle top evenly with skim milk powder. Bake 1 hour. Cool. Refrigerate until set. (⅓ of entire pie equals 1 fruit.)

FRUIT PIE

1 large apple
1 large pear
¼ fresh pineapple
½ cup blueberries
2 envelopes unflavored gelatin
1 can or bottle low-calorie lemon soda
½ teaspoon cinnamon
1 envelope artificial sweetener, or equivalent
¼ cup dry skim milk powder

Preheat oven to 350°. Core apple and pear and slice into pie plate. Add cut-up pineapple, and blueberries. Dissolve gelatin in ¼ cup of the lemon soda. Boil remaining soda and add to soda-gelatin mixture. Cool. Sprinkle fruit with cinnamon and sweetener, and pour soda-gelatin mixture over all. Sprinkle powdered milk evenly on top. Bake for 1 hour. Cool. Refrigerate until set. (¼ entire pie equals 1 fruit.)

BEVERAGES

THINK THIN COCKTAIL

1 cup water
1 envelope beef bouillon powder, or 1 cube
¼ teaspoon Worcestershire sauce
1 lemon slice
½ teaspoon minced parsley

Dissolve bouillon concentrate in boiling water. Cool. Add Worcestershire sauce. Serve on the rocks in an Old-Fashioned glass. Sprinkle with parsley and float lemon slice on top. (Good when entertaining and everyone else is drinking alcoholic beverages.) *Unlimited.*

MILK SHAKE

1 cup skim milk
½ teaspoon vanilla extract
1 teaspoon instant coffee powder
1 envelope artificial sweetener, or equivalent
3 ice cubes, crushed

Mix all ingredients in blender except ice. Add ice gradually. Serve immediately. (Equals ½ skim milk requirement.)

FRUIT MILK SHAKE

1 cup skim milk
½ teaspoon vanilla extract
1 fruit (6 strawberries, 1 peach, etc.)
1 envelope artificial sweetener, or equivalent
3 ice cubes, crushed

Mix all ingredients in blender except ice. Add ice gradually. Serve immediately. (Equals ½ skim milk requirement and 1 fruit.)

SUMMER FRUIT COOLER

1 peach, peeled and cut up
½ canteloupe, peeled and cut up
½ recipe Orange Sherbet (See Index.)
1 envelope artificial sweetener, or equivalent

Mix thoroughly in blender. (Equals 2 fruits and ½ milk requirement.)

MILK DELIGHT

1 cup skim milk
½ can or bottle any flavor low-calorie soda
1 envelope artificial sweetener, or equivalent
3 crushed ice cubes

Mix all ingredients in blender except ice. Add ice gradually. Serve immediately.

SPICED GINGER ALE

1 can low-calorie ginger ale
¼ teaspoon cinnamon
¼ teaspoon nutmeg
3 whole cloves or ¼ teaspoon ground cloves

Boil all together until fizz is gone. Serve hot or cold.

ROOT BEER COOLER

1 cup skim milk
Low-calorie root beer
1 scoop Pineapple Sherbet (See Index.)

Mix milk and root beer. Spoon in sherbet. Serve in tall glass with straw.

CAPPUCCINO

½ cup skim milk heated to just under boiling point
1 level teaspoon instant coffee dissolved in
    ½ cup boiling water
                or
½ cup hot percolated coffee
1 stick cinnamon
Dash of allspice
Artificial sweetener if desired

ut milk into blender and blend until foamy. Pour hot
ɔffee into mug. Spoon or pour foamed milk over coffee.
Put in cinnamon stick. Sprinkle with allspice. Add sweetener
if desired.

EGG CREAM

1 cup skim milk
½ can or bottle any flavor low-calorie soda

Mix thoroughly. (Equals ½ daily skim milk requirement.)

BLOODY MARY

½ cup tomato juice
Dash Tabasco
¼ teaspoon Worcestershire sauce
½ teaspoon lemon juice
Fresh ground black pepper
Salt

Mix all ingredients. Serve on the rocks in an Old-Fashioned glass. (Good when others are drinking alcoholic
beverages.)

HORSE'S NECK

Club soda
Long curving strip of lemon peel

Serve in highball glass with ice. (Good when others are
drinking alcoholic beverages.) *Unlimited*.

Note: The following beverages are *unlimited:*

Water

Coffee

Tea

Club soda

Quinine water

Bouillon (onion, beef, chicken, vegetable) made from cube or powder.

INDEX

(An asterisk following entry indicates recipe)

269